Aircraft
OF THE ACES

Legends of World War 2

Featuring the acclaimed artwork of Iain Wyllie

Aircraft OF THE ACES

Legends of World War 2

Featuring the acclaimed artwork of Iain Wyllie

Compiled by Tony Holmes

Forewords by Air Commodore Peter Brothers
CBE, DSO, DFC and Bar

and

Colonel Clarence E 'Bud' Anderson

First published in Great Britain in 2000 by Osprey Publishing,
Elms Court, Chapel Way, Botley, Oxford, OX2 9LP
E-mail: info@ospreypublishing.com

UK EDITION ISBN 1 84176 155 9
USA EDITION ISBN 1 84176 156 7

Written and edited by Tony Holmes
Page design by Rebecca Smart
Layout by Mark Holt
Cover Artwork by Iain Wyllie
Aircraft Profiles by Chris Davey, the late Keith Fretwell, Robert 'Buba'
    Grudzien, Mark Styling, Tom Tullis and John Weal
Scale Drawings by Mark Styling and Arthur Bentley

Origination by Valhaven Ltd, Isleworth, UK
Printed by Ajanta Offset, New Delhi, India

00 01 02 03 04   10 9 8 7 6 5 4 3 2 1

EDITOR'S NOTE

To make the best-selling *Aircraft of the Aces* series as authoritative as possible,
the editor would be interested in hearing from any individual who may have
relevant photographs, documentation or first-hand experiences relating to
the elite pilots, and their aircraft, of the various theatres of war. Any material
used will be credited to its original source. Please write to Tony Holmes at
10 Prospect Road, Sevenoaks, Kent, TN13 3UA, Great Britain, or by e-mail
at; tony.holmes@osprey-jets.freeserve.co.uk

ACKNOWLEDGEMENTS

Firstly, the authors would like to thank both 'Bud' Anderson and
'Pete' Brothers for supplying the forewords which so accurately set
the scene for what follows within this volume.

Tony Holmes is also greatly indebted to the following individuals
for supplying words and photos for this book at very short notice;
John Weal, Henry Sakaida, Wojtek Matusiak, Zdenek Hurt, Jiri
Rajlich, Peter Hinchliffe, Fritz Rumpelhardt, Peter Arnold, Jerry
Scutts, Phil Jarrett, Hill Goodspeed at the National Museum of
Naval Aviation, Peter Mersky, Jim Sullivan, Doug Seigfried at the
Tailhook Association, John Stanaway, George Mellinger, Nigel
Eastaway, Barrett Tillman, Robert Forsyth, Eddie Creek, Chris
Thomas, Roger Freeman, Dwayne Tabbatts, Dennis Kucera, Andy
Saunders, Simon Watson, William Hess, Sam Sox, Barry Ketley, Kari
Stenman, Norman Franks and Ian Phillips.

Finally, Tony Holmes wishes the thank his wife Katy for her
quick-fire typing, and he promises that one day all Osprey
contributors will have access to a PC and floppy discs!

The authors also acknowledge the use of brief extracts from the
following essential reference works:

Arise to Conquer by Ian Gleed
Joe Foss, Flying Marine by Joe Foss and Walter Simmons
German Fighter Ace Hans-Joachim Marseille by Franz Kurowski
Great American Fighter Aces by Dan Bauer
I Flew for the Führer by Heinz Knoke
Aces Against Germany - The American Aces Speak, Volume II
    by Eric Hammel
Schnaufer - Ace of Diamonds by Peter Hinchliffe
Tumult in the Clouds by James Goodson
To Fly and Fight by Clarence E 'Bud' Anderson with
    Joseph P Hamelin
Fighter Aces of the USA by Raymond F Toliver and
    Trevor J Constable
Battle over Bavaria by Robert Forsyth with Jerry Scutts
Combat Kill by Hugh Morgan and Jürgen Seibel

For a catalogue of all titles published by Osprey Military and Aviation please write to:

Osprey Direct UK, P.O. Box 140,
Wellingborough, Northants NN8 4ZA, UK
E-mail: info@ospreydirect.co.uk

Osprey Direct USA, P.O. Box 130,
Sterling Heights, MI 48311-0130, USA
E-mail: info@ospreydirectusa.com

Visit Osprey at www.ospreypublishing.com

CONTENTS

FOREWORD

Happily retired in rural Berkshire, the invitation to write a foreword to this book has jolted my mind back to the days of World War 2, with its dramas and tragedies, its comedies and merriment and, above all, its friendships. Much as been written about the conflict, and particularly about the Battle of Britain – those days in 1940 when the future of this country hung by a thread under the threat of invasion, that thread being the Royal Air Force and particularly the pilots and aircraft of Fighter Command, heavily outnumbered as they were by the Luftwaffe.

It is surprising that the passage of years seems in no way to have diminished the interest shown in that Battle. As its title implies, this book is a welcome addition to a well-established and highly successful series following in the footsteps of and matching the high standards set by its predecessors. The combination of Iain Wyllie's excellent artwork coupled with contemporary photographs and first-hand accounts by some of the pilots involved make for fascinating reading. Those who had shot down five aircraft became known as aces, and some of them are portrayed here.

My childhood was spent playing with model aircraft and reading about my heroes, the aces of World War 1 – Ball, Mannock, McCudden, I knew them all. Determined to fly, I flew solo aged 16, until I was stopped by a Government Order after the other 16-year-old killed himself. Angered at the time by having to fly with an instructor until 17, I was lucky for he was a First War fighter pilot and he taught me many tricks. That, and the fact that I joined the RAF in January 1936, meant that when war came I was well experienced. This probably saved my life, and certainly contributed to what success I had.

So it was that I both endured and enjoyed the Battle. The moments of intense fear when outnumbered, heavily attacked and fighting for your life, of anger when shot-up by being stupid enough to fall into a simple trap laid by enemy fighters, and the utter surprise and glee when a short burst of fire caused the enemy aircraft to fall apart in the air. These were the moments of life in those hectic days.

But life could not be taken seriously under such circumstances. To do so would have imperilled morale, for our situation could hardly be regarded as blissful. So in my first squadron, No 32 at Biggin Hill, we adopted schoolboyish names – 'The Baron' was John Worrall, our CO, 'Red Knight' was Mike Crossley, 'A' Flight Commander, I was 'Blue Peter', 'B' Flight Commander, Duckenfield became 'von Dukenfeldt' and Rose 'Beacon', and so it went on.

War was a game and treated as such, to fly, to fight, to laugh, to drink and not to cry. Losses sad, but not dwelt on. Later, when I transferred to a squadron which had suffered heavy losses, I realised the importance of all this to morale. In our never expressed private thoughts we realised that we were engaged in a battle for survival, and to lose meant death or the salt mines and your wife in a German brothel. So we fought and won despite the odds.

But I digress. This book is not a philosophical survey of fighter pilots, rather an impressively illustrated book with a text enhanced by the inclusion of personal accounts by the pilots engaged in the actions depicted, expanded from and more detailed than their official combat reports made at the time. This is backed up with brief biographies of the pilots involved and detailed technical explanations of their aircraft, as well as contemporary photographs and a full-colour side-view profile.

For the historian, the student of air warfare, the Battle of Britain 'buff' or for those merely interested in a good aviation read, this book is a 'must'.

Pete Brothers

Peter Brothers CBE, DSO, DFC and Bar
Air Commodore, RAF Retired
April 2000

FOREWORD

After all these years, I continue to be amazed at the widespread public interest in World War 2 aviation, and the pilots who became aces during that gigantic and costly conflict. This book will certainly nourish that interest. The collection of Ian Wyllie's paintings from the *Aircraft of the Aces* series does a fantastic job in capturing the action during those deadly exciting times in the air. Fighter aircraft of World War 2 were often very colourful, and are vividly displayed in this collection. There was a great deal of individualism expressed in the way these aircraft were painted, especially among the aces.

First, we must again define 'What is an ace?' One of the dictionary definitions for this expression is that an ace is an expert at what ever one does. Here, we are talking about fighter pilots who destroy five or more enemy aircraft in air-to-air combat. Aces were few in number when compared to the total number of fighter pilots engaged in combat, yet, remarkably, these individuals downed by far the greatest percentage of the aircraft destroyed in aerial combat.

The traits of a good fighter pilot are many and probably indivisible. I have often contemplated what made the difference between a good fighter pilot and a great fighter pilot when all circumstances appeared equal. It occurs to me that it is something special in the personal make up of the individual - call it a fighting spirit, an inner drive, aggression, motivation or whatever, but you certainly had to have the desire to enter into aerial combat time and time again to survive. Having said all this, I also agree that I had a great deal of luck in being at the right place at the right time to finish two combat tours without a scratch!

The personal names painted on the aircraft vary. You can find just about anything you can imagine – names of sweethearts and wives, nicknames, national symbols, nude female figures and so on. I picked the name 'Old Crow' and painted it on a P-39 while in training. It was later worn on all my P-51s during my tours with the 357th Fighter Group in the ETO. There was even an F-105D called *OLD CROW II* during the later stages of the Vietnam War.

I tell my non-drinking friends that the name was inspired by the smartest bird that flies in the sky, but my drinking buddies all know it was named after that good old Kentucky straight bourbon whiskey! My wife likes to kid around when talking about this name, and suggests that most pilots name their aeroplanes after their sweetheart or wife, so what must people think is going on here!

My desire to fly goes back as far as I can remember, and when I finally became a pilot, I wanted to be a fighter pilot. World War 2 had everything to do with making these things come true, and when I became a combat fighter pilot, naturally I wanted to be among the elite few – the aces. World War 2 was a total thing. The entire country was solidly behind the war effort, and there was tremendous patriotism. We were all mostly young men just doing what we had to do.

At first when I became an ace I felt like I was just doing my job, but later I had a great sense of satisfaction with all the appreciation that was shown. After the war that was all quickly forgotten, but now many years later there seems to be a new wave of interest, respect and true appreciation for what our fighting men did for the free world during World War 2.

CE 'Bud' Anderson

Clarence E 'Bud' Anderson
Colonel, USAF Retired
April 2000

INTRODUCTION BY THE ARTIST

I have been drawing for as long as I can remember, longer in fact, as I have a drawing inscribed on the back 'racing car by Iain, aged 2 yrs 4 mths'.

My first recollection of matters aeronautical was at about the age of four, when I was extremely impressed by the amount of noise made by a Boston as it flew low over the house. Living as we did within a few miles of the Shorts factory, we were used to seeing a wide variety of their products, as well as the usual miscellany of military aircraft, both British and American, which abounded at that time.

Another vivid memory which impressed itself on my young mind was of kneeling on the back seat of the family Wolsely 9

on the road that ran past Nutts Corner airfield, watching a Lancaster taxying along behind us as it was marshalled to a dispersal across the road from the airfield.

Later, in the late 1940s and 1950s, we holidayed regularly at Castlerock in County Londonderry. Nearby were the airfields of Eglinton and Ballykelly, and we were frequently entertained by

RIGHT The artist gets up close to his subject matter, which in this case is a No 72 Sqn Wessex HC 2, based at RAF Aldergrove

BELOW Just to prove that I can produce artwork that features aircraft aside from fighters, this painting depicts famous German bomber pilot Oberst Hajo Herrmann's Ju 88. The artwork was commissioned in 1998 by Kestrel Publishing, and 300 numbered prints were produced that were signed by the highly-decorated Herrmann

A rivet-counter's dream – this artwork of a No 25 Sqn Fury II was reproduced as a gatefold

Barracudas carrying out dive-bombing practice and Sea Furies blasting past the beach at low level and high speed.

From the hills above Ballykelly, Shackletons were spotted through binoculars as they took off and set course out over the Atlantic until they dwindled to the five dots of engines and fuselage far to the west.

My first flight was in 1950 in a BEA Viking from Nutts Corner to Northolt, which was a real thrill at that time. Throughout school and college years, as probably the last generation to remain undistracted by television, my friends and I built and flew model aircraft. Our houses reeked regularly with the acid-drop smell of cellulose nitrate dope, and we seemed to spend a lot of time chewing dried balsa cement from finger tips criss-crossed with the marks of the razor blades used to cut out balsa wood structures.

Without really realising it, we gained a working knowledge of empirical aerodynamics – the effects of CG (Centre of Gravity) positions, angles of incidence, thrust lines, stability etc, as we designed our own models. I always preferred free-flight models as, compared to control line models, they flew unfettered in their natural element.

In my mid-twenties I embarked on flying lessons, being taught by one of Shorts test pilots – the years of model flying were of unexpected benefit, as I found that flying full-sized aircraft came quite naturally.

After some years when I was otherwise engaged, I picked up my brushes again, this time to paint my other favourite subject – the sea and fast sailing ships. Water in motion is one of the most difficult subjects to portray convincingly. Quite apart from

understanding the forces which produce the physical form of waves on the deep oceans, or breakers on the coast, the artist has to deal with translucency, reflection, transparency and foam patterns.

The sailing ships themselves also require a technical knowledge of rigging and sail handling – that is to say the amount and set of the sails carried in different conditions of wind and sea. The hull of the ship also has a characteristic motion dependent on its course relative to the wind direction, and therefore the direction of the seas. The five years I had earlier spent studying naval architecture were bearing fruit!

Also of help was my early interest in meteorology, a study which was to be useful when I took part in competition, flying radio-controlled thermal soarers. This proved useful in relating cloud types and sea states with different windspeeds for my marine paintings and also, naturally, for aviation painting.

Apart from the different types of cloud which form at various altitudes and in different combinations, it is interesting to note that clouds in tropical areas have characteristic differences to clouds in temperate regions.

When painting aircraft, the lighting is all important. The main source of light is, of course, the sun, but the amount of cloud beneath the aircraft is important as it will reflect light up into the shadows, lightening them. At higher altitudes the sky overhead can be a very dark blue-black. In this instance, the sun acts as a spotlight, providing highlights, and the underside can be brilliantly lit by reflected light from cloud layers below. The plot thickens if the aircraft is in natural metal finish, as this also reduces the depth of shadows in itself, as well as reflecting colours – the degree of polish also exaggerates the reflected tones. Therefore, it is quite possible to look at a photograph of an aircraft in flight with the background removed and fairly accurately estimate the atmospheric conditions.

Quite often, after painting a sky, I am rather loathe to add a large aircraft in the foreground so I reduce its size greatly – this can be very effective, as it creates a great sense of space and atmosphere. Unfortunately, most clients usually want the aircraft large with the background sky just that – a background. Perhaps this is due to the influence of air-to-air photography, which in most cases features aircraft in close-up portraiture. Personally, I would like to see more paintings of skies which include aircraft, rather than vice versa. Quite a number of paintings by the late Roy Nockolds were done in this style, and these influenced my early thinking of aviation art.

Earlier, the ships in my marine paintings gradually diminished in size until latterly they disappeared altogether, leaving a breaking wave or coastal scene to become the main focus. The appeal of the painting then relied on atmosphere alone. There can be few among us who have not sat or stood at the edge of the sea, enjoying the pleasure of watching the waves breaking and the changing light in the sky and on the surface of the water.

Of course there are, equally, occasions when a sense of drama is required to portray action, power or speed, and this is particularly true of cover art. Here, the composition must be kept simple and uncluttered, giving a clear flavour of what the book is about.

Backgrounds, especially at low altitude, are kept low-key or blurred in the direction of flight – nothing 'stops' an aircraft quicker than a pin-sharp background. If the viewpoint is at

ground level then, normally, more attention is paid to the surrounding land or seascape, but if the viewpoint is at the same altitude as the aircraft, it is somewhat incongruous to portray a 'chocolate box' village of thatched cottages suffused in golden sunlight and painted in minute detail. Flying low, even at 150 knots, one can only form a general impression of the terrain below. Too much sharp detail in a painting equates to a photograph taken at 1/1000 sec – a frozen moment in time, and totally static.

The research required to portray an incident or action can be extensive, encompassing altitude, weather conditions, direction of flight related to the sun, time of day and time of year. This is quite apart from details of the main aircraft type, mark, paint scheme, markings, non-standard fittings and so on. Any opponents shown have to be correctly depicted – today, we are fortunate in having a vast amount of research on which to draw, and it is often possible to pin down the actual details of aircraft and pilots from both sides of a given combat. With an action painting, it is not necessary to add vast amounts of detail. In fact this detracts from the immediacy of the painting. I will leave this approach to the days when I produced large airbrushed gatefolds, when screwheads and, occasionally, rivets were counted!

It is relatively straightforward to illustrate aircraft in flight. The real difficulty is involving the viewer emotionally in what is happening, and what it is like to be there. This is the *real* art of aviation painting.

More rivet-counting. P-47D-1 Thunderbolt 42-7945 was flown by five-kill ace Lt Spiros 'Steve' Pissanos, who was universally known as 'The Greek' to his squadronmates in the 334th FS/4th FG at Debden in 1943-44

INTRODUCTION BY THE AUTHOR

By simple definition of being the best of the best, the aces of the various conflicts of the 20th century have enjoyed their fair share of press adoration and propaganda. And rightly so, as the feats of the Marseilles, Hartmanns, McCampbells and Pattles of World War 2 reveal unprecedented levels of airmanship tempered with raw courage.

Unsurprisingly, given their predilection for the dramatic hero, it was the French who first used the term 'ace' to describe successful aviators in the first year of World War 1. With trench warfare well and truly established by then, and hundreds of thousands of French troops being slaughtered in relative anonymity at the front, the national press looked to the skies to find a replacement for their heroes of the past – the cavalrymen. Instead of being saddled to a charger, the 'hussars' of the Great War were now strapped into an often equally temperamental fighting scout. Indeed, the frailty of

these early aircraft was to prematurely end the career of the world's first ace, Roland Garros (he claimed six victories but only three of these were confirmed), when mechanical failure forced him down behind German lines on 19 April 1915.

By then, however, French journalists and publicists alike had already equated Garros's exploits with previous French military heroes. Fighting as an individual thousands of feet above the muddy trenches, his feats could be easily divorced from the mass destruction on the ground. These aerial battles received much coverage in the press, and quickly boosted flagging civilian morale on both sides of the front.

The hands say it all. Just returned from yet another successful sortie during the Battle of Britain, JG 2's then ace of aces, Oberleutnant Helmut Wick, describes his most recent success over the Channel to his *Gruppenkommandeur*, Major Hennig Strümpell, at Beaumont-le-Roger in the autumn of 1940 (*via John Weal*)

An early escape for the future 'Star of Afrika'. An apparently unconcerned Oberfähnrich Hans-Joachim Marseille of I./JG 27 cheerfully points to battle damage to the cowling of his Bf 109E-4/Trop. This photograph was taken at the *Gruppe's* Castel Benito base, in Libya, during the spring of 1941 (*via John Weal*)

The first officially recognised ace was, appropriately, a Frenchman. Eugene Gilbert scored five victories in the spring of 1915 flying a two-seat Morane Type 'L' parasol monoplane. He was one of a handful of Allied pilots to initially gain the ascendancy over the Western Front, although this situation was soon reversed with the appearance of the legendary Fokker E-I *Eindekker*, flown by pilots of the calibre of Immelmann and Boelcke. These men were the first true fighter tacticians, revolutionising air combat through the creation of a series of combat manoeuvres that are still employed by today's frontline fast jet pilots.

German aces dominated the skies, and the headlines, for much of World War 1, and today the world's most famous ace remains *Rittmeister Freiherr* Manfred von Richthofen, better known as the 'Red Baron'. Other notable aces from the conflict included 'Mick' Mannock, Billy Bishop and Albert Ball of the Royal Flying Corps (RFC), Frenchmen Georges Guynemer, René Fonck and Charles Nungesser, Americans Frank Luke and Eddie Rickenbacker, and German legends Ernst Udet, Werner Voss and Bruno Loerzer.

The myth of the ace was perpetuated during the 1920s and 30s through both factual and fictional accounts. Prolific British author Capt W E Johns captivated a generation of teenage boys with his *Biggles* stories, his central character having been an 'RFC Camel ace' on the Western Front. Much biographical and autobiographical literature on aces also appeared at around this time, with one of the more famous titles being *King of the Air Fighters*, which described the career of ranking British World War 1 ace 'Mick' Mannock. The book was written in 1934 by fellow ace

Ira 'Taffy' Jones, who had been both a squadronmate and friend of Mannock up until the latter pilot's death in action in July 1918. The style of the time is perfectly reflected in the following quote taken from the book's preface;

'To the modern schoolboy, Edward Mannock is the most inspiring figure in the Great War. His achievements may serve as a beacon to them; a guide along the path of personal endeavour and Duty to their State.'

Such rhetoric rang strongly in the ears of impressionable youth who would soon become the next generation of fighter pilots. And their 'Duty to State' would be put to the ultimate test with the militarisation of Germany in the 1930s, the power-posturing of the Fascists in Italy and the imperialist expansion of the Japanese in the Far East.

That such works by Ira Jones and numerous other veteran pilots planted a seed in the minds of future aces is beyond doubt. 'My childhood was spent playing with model aircraft and reading about my heroes, the aces of the First War – Ball, Mannock, McCudden, I knew them all', is how triple ace 'Pete' Brothers describes his formative years in the foreword for this volume. He was not alone in poring over the exploits of the aces.

'I read everything I could find about my heroes of aviation, such men as Barker, Bishop, McLeod Mannock and McCudden. I

A quartet of successful Typhoon pilots from No 609 Sqn. Each of these men was awarded the DFC in the autumn of 1943. They are, from left to right, Flg Off 'Mony' van Lierde (6 kills), Plt Off 'Pinkie' Stark (6 kills), Flg Off 'Windmill Charlie Demoulin and Flt Lt Johnny Baldwin (16 kills) (*via Chris Thomas*)

suppose, like many others, I was most thrilled by the tales of the great fighter aces, but I never supposed that there would be a convenient war which would allow me to take part in similar battles'. The words of future Canadian ace Johnny Kent.

This fascination for aces was also rife in isolationist America during this period, as ETO ace Richard E Turner described in his autobiography *Mustang Pilot*;

'As a young sprout, I had been an avid consumer of all tales and stories, fact or fiction, concerning the adventures of that swashbuckling gallant band of warriors who cut their niche in history fighting resolutely in the skies through World War 1 as fighter pilots. Their exploits captured my imagination at an early age; even now at the threshold of war the desire to join their ranks proved irresistible. My goal was to be a fighter pilot.'

Motivated by the feats of the aces of the Great War, and flying fighter aircraft that were far more effective in their designed role thanks to improvements in engine power, airframe design and weaponry, pilots itched to get at the enemy. Many German and Japanese fighter pilots had a combat edge over their rivals in the early stages of the war due to their participation in earlier conflicts in Spain and China respectively. And a number of aces had been created during the fighting in both countries, pilots debuting the new generation of monoplane fighters such as the German Bf 109, Russian I-16 and Japanese Ki-97.

The *Blitzkrieg* into Poland in September 1939, followed by the war in the west in May 1940, soon meant that Allied fighter pilots had also experienced the stark realities of modern aerial combat. In northern Europe, the Soviet invasion of Finland also resulted in a series of bitter aerial engagements, and war would

continue to be waged between these two countries until 1944. Finally, the Italian declaration of war on Britain and France in June 1940 opened up new theatres for action over the deserts of North Africa and the warm waters of the Mediterranean.

Just as in World War 1, the Germans coveted their aces, with the early exploits of men such as Mölders and Wick dominating the Nazi-controlled press. In Britain, the RAF once again played down the idea of aces, as it had done over two decades earlier. 'Better to favour the team than the individual' was the official policy, and the effects of this can still be seen today, with successful aces from World War 2 denigrating their role in the conflict for fear of being labelled 'line-shooters' by their contemporaries.

With the surprise German invasion of the USSR in June 1941 and the Japanese bombing of the US Pacific Fleet in Pearl Harbor six months later, World War 2 became a truly global conflict. The importance of air power, and the mastery of the skies, was understood by both sides, and the opportunities for men to make their mark in fighter aircraft abounded – as will be graphically revealed in the following chapters of this book.

SERIES SUCCESS

Since the autumn of 1994, many of these engagements between pilots motivated by 'personal endeavour and Duty to their State', to paraphrase 'Taffy' Jones, have been recounted in the *Aircraft of the Aces* series, from which this volume is derived.

When I devised the *Aircraft of the Aces* series for Osprey Aviation Publishing, my primary motivation was to bring the stories of the various elite pilots to life in a package that was affordable to all aviation enthusiasts. In the past, worthy tomes on aces had been produced either in encyclopaedic form, as pilot biographies/autobiographies or as part of an overall unit history. These books tended to be expensive, text heavy and with black and white illustrations only. The writing style also differed greatly due to the disparate nature of the books, their various publishers and the period in which they were released.

Inspired by previous Osprey series such as the *Aircams* and *Air Wars* of the 1970s, and using a modern mix of artwork, period photography and text commissioned and written to a series brief, the first two titles in the *Aircraft of the Aces* series were launched in the autumn of 1994. Since then, a further 33 books have appeared, and over 400,000 Osprey-imprinted volumes have been sold to

Few photos better demonstrate American mastery of the skies in the Pacific than this official shot of leading US Navy ace, Cdr David McCampbell, sat in his F6F-5 Hellcat *Minsi III* on the deck of USS *Essex* on 25 October 1944. The previous day, he had downed nine Japanese fighters during the course of a single sortie (*via the National Museum of Naval Aviation*)

date. In addition to these 'home brand' books, the *Aircraft of the Aces* series has also been published in Spanish, Italian, Polish, French and Japanese language editions, proving that the fascination for elite pilots, and their aircraft, is universal.

Two of the key ingredients in the success of this series can be found in abundance within this volume, namely the artwork (both cover and profile) and the first-hand accounts from the aces themselves. Examining the artwork first, each title has featured a specially-commissioned cover painting by Iain Wyllie, and these have consistently set the scene for the books' content.

As his introduction to this particular volume reveals, Iain is a stickler when it comes to getting things right. Indeed, I never fail to be amazed when he recounts his latest tale on how he has ascertained the accuracy of a certain element of the artwork. Perhaps my all time favourite concerns his ringing up of the archivist at Trinity House to find out what colours the bands on the lighthouse at the base of The Needles were in November 1940 (said lighthouse can just be made out in the painting featured on page 31, chapter four). Such research is the hallmark of a great artist.

The profile artists have also made a considerable contribution to the series as a whole, and only a fraction of the 1300+ artworks they have created specially for Osprey are on display in this book. Again craftsmen of the highest quality, through their endeavours (working from references provided by the various authors) they have succeeded in turning what is an essentially 'black and white' war for those of us studying it some 60 years after the event, into a subject full of colour and vibrancy. Indeed, the only thing that can match cover and profile art of 'Bud' Anderson's *OLD CROW* or Hans-Joachim Jabs' 'Nordpol-Paula' for sheer impact are the accounts from the aces themselves of the actions that these aircraft were embroiled in.

Throughout the life of the *Aircraft of the Aces* series, I have always impressed upon the contributing authors the importance of first-hand accounts. Their inclusion has allowed readers to be sat in a P-38G over the Aegean Sea as Bill Leverette cut a swathe through the ranks of Ju 87Ds off the coast of Rhodes, or accompanied the great Werner Mölders as he took to his parachute after his *Emil* was mortally struck by machine gun fire from an unseen French D.520 north-east of Paris.

Around these accounts, the authors have skilfully described the exploits of literally thousands of aces from World War 1, World War 2 and the Korean War. Supported by carefully chosen archival photography and thoroughly researched artwork, the overall *Aircraft of the Aces* package has proven irresistible for enthusiasts across the globe. I hope that you will also be inspired to seek out other titles in this series after viewing Iain Wyllie's artwork and reading the compelling first-hand combat accounts contained within this volume.

BOSOM PATROL

'I had soon set the Me 109 on fire. This made me even more unpopular with his squadronmates, and the excitement of the dogfight grew in intensity as four of them attacked me from different directions.'

No 32 Sqn's 'B' Flight commander, Flt Lt 'Pete' Brothers, scored his first victories in the final days of the *Blitzkrieg*, before going on to achieve 'acedom' in the Battle of Britain (*'Pete' Brothers*)

'It was Saturday, 20 July 1940. Following what was becoming normal practice, we deployed to Hawkinge, on the Kent coast, from Biggin Hill, where we spent a quiet morning and what turned into a noisy afternoon.

'About 5 pm, No 32 Sqn was ordered to patrol over the convoy *BOSOM*, which was some ten miles east of Dover, steaming north-eastwards. Led by Sqn Ldr John "The Baron" Worrall, the nine of us, happy to be relieved of the boredom of waiting around on the ground, took off to perform the dull job of patrolling up and down a line of ships, which we duly did for a while. Over the convoy, we were joined by ten Hurricanes from No 615 Sqn and, to the west of us, nine Spitfires of No 610 Sqn were also flying their patrol at a higher altitude.

'Towards the end of our patrol, "Sappa" (our ground control) warned us of enemy aircraft approaching from the south-east, and sure enough there they were – a force of at least 50 aircraft, comprised of Ju 87s escorted by Me 109s and Me 110 Jaguars. Happily, we were "up sun" of them, and I think unseen.

As the Ju 87s started their dive, "The Baron" led the six aircraft of Green and Red Sections down to bounce them. I was about to follow with Sub Lt Gordon Bulmer and Sgt Bill Higgins when I saw about 30 Me 109s taking an unwelcome interest in us, so I swung Blue Section around to attack them. This seemed to offend them so much that they picked on my section of three Hurricanes instead, and from what had been a peaceful sky suddenly erupted into a confused melée of aircraft swirling round firing at anything in sight.

'One of the Messerschmitts overshot me, and I managed more by luck than judgement to get on his tail. Opening fire in five-second bursts at a distance of 150 yards and closing, I had soon set the Me 109 on fire. This made me even more unpopular with his squadronmates, and the excitement of the dogfight grew in

Iain Wyllie

On 29 July 1940 a Fox Film Unit photographer shot a number of stills at Hawkinge whilst his colleagues were busy making a series of instructional films for the RAF. Some of the images he captured that day are easily amongst the best photos taken during the Battle of Britain, showing pilots at readiness between sorties. His subjects were No 32 Sqn's 'B' Flight, forward based at Hawkinge from Biggin Hill. The seven pilots seen here resting at dispersal are, from left to right, Plt Offs R F Smythe, Keith Gillman and J E Proctor, Flt Lt P M Brothers and Plt Offs D H Grice, P M Gardner and A F Eckford (*via John Weal*)

intensity as four of them attacked me from different directions. I was not happy with such unfriendly attention, and made a head-on attack on two of them before running out of ammunition. As I wheeled round to guard my tail, I found that the sky had cleared and there was not an aircraft in sight – no friends, no foes, nothing. Feeling lonely and vulnerable, I made for home.

'On arrival at Hawkinge I found that "The Baron" had been badly shot-up and crash-landed near the airfield, fortunately with only slight injuries. Worse, Sub Lt Bulmer was missing. He had been with us but 20 days, and had little combat experience. Many years later I learned that he had been shot down by the ace Oberleutnant Josef "Pips" Priller of I./JG 51. And although Bulmer had succeeded in bailing out of his stricken Hurricane, he had drowned.

'From subsequent checks by Intelligence Staff on No 32 Sqn, it seems between us we had successfully destroyed one Ju 87, two Me 109s and three Me 110 Jaguars. What a noisy afternoon it had been.'

This famous photograph was taken by the official RAF Biggin Hill station photographer on the afternoon of Thursday, 15 August 1940 – the day of the largest ever aerial assault on Britain by the Luftwaffe. No 32 Sqn was scrambled three times during the course of the day, and this shot was taken as the unit's nine surviving Hurricane Is recovered at the sector station following the completion of the final mission (*via Phil Jarrett*)

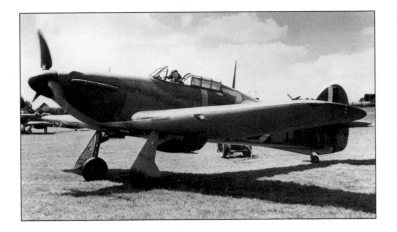

Another in the sequence of Fox photos from 29 July 1940, this shot shows Plt Off Rupert Smythe about to taxy away from the dispersal in Hurricane I P3522 after receiving the order to scramble. He used this fighter to destroy two Bf 109Es (plus a third unconfirmed) off Deal on 4 July and a Do 17 (claimed as a 'Do 215' by the pilot) again off Deal/Dover on 12 August (*via Phil Jarrett*)

PILOT BIOGRAPHY – 'PETE' BROTHERS

Lancastrian Peter Malam 'Pete' Brothers joined No 32 Sqn at RAF Biggin Hill in October 1936, where he flew Gauntlet II biplane fighters until the first Hurricane Is arrived at the No 11 Group station exactly two years later. By then a highly experienced fighter pilot, and flight commander, Brothers first saw action as a result of the German *Blitzkrieg* into Western Europe in May 1940. Embroiled in the Battle of Britain following the surrender of France, he remained in the thick of the action by joining No 257 Sqn in early September following No 32 Sqn's posting out of the frontline. Flt Lt Brothers was awarded a Distinguished Flying Cross (DFC) just prior to leaving his beloved No 32 Sqn.

With his score standing at 12 kills, Brothers briefly served as an instructer in early 1941 before being promoted to squadron leader and tasked with forming the Australian-manned No 457 Sqn, equipped with Spitfires. He was to see continual service in Supermarine fighters throughout the remaining war years during a succession of frontline postings, leading No 602 Sqn in 1942, the Tangmere Wing the following year and finally the Exeter and Culmhead Wings in 1944. By VE-Day, now Wg Cdr Brothers had increased his score to 16 destroyed, 1 probable and 3 damaged, and been awarded a bar to his DFC and a Distinguished Service Order (DSO).

Postwar, he remained in the RAF until retiring with the rank of air commodore in 1973. Several years later, Brothers was subsequently elected Master of the Guild of Air Pilots and Air Navigators, his City of London Livery Company. Still very active within the Battle of Britain Pilots' Association today, 'Pete' Brothers lives with his wife Annette and dog Spindle in Eastbury.

SPECIFICATION

Hawker Hurricane Mk I
(all dimensions and performance data for Hurricane Mk I)

TYPE:	single-engined monoplane fighter
ACCOMMODATION:	pilot
DIMENSIONS:	length 31 ft 5 in (9.58 m) wingspan 40 ft 0 in (12.19 m) height 13 ft 0 in (3.96 m)
WEIGHTS:	empty 4982 lb (2260 kg) maximum take-off 7490 lb (3397 kg)
PERFORMANCE:	maximum speed 324 mph (521 kmh) range 600 miles (965 km) powerplant Rolls-Royce Merlin I/II/III output 1030 hp (768 kW)
ARMAMENT:	eight 0.303 in machine guns in wings
FIRST FLIGHT DATE:	6 November 1935
OPERATORS:	Australia, Belgium, Canada, Finland, France, The Netherlands East Indies, Romania, South Africa, UK, Yugoslavia
PRODUCTION:	3843

The Hurricane's arrival in the frontline in December 1937 saw the RAF finally make the jump from biplane to monoplane fighter. The aircraft owed much to Hawker's ultimate biplane design, the Fury, both types being built around an internal 'skeleton' of four wire-braced alloy and steel tube longerons – this structure was renowned for both its simplicity of construction and durability. The Hurricane also benefited from Hawker's long-standing partnership with Rolls-Royce, whose newly-developed Merlin I engine proved to be the ideal powerplant. Toting eight 0.303 in machine guns, and capable of speeds in excess of 300 mph, the Hurricane I was the world's most advanced fighter when issued to the RAF. Although technically eclipsed by the Spitfire come the summer of 1940, Hurricanes nevertheless outnumbered the former type during the Battle of Britain by three to one, and actually downed more Luftwaffe aircraft than the Supermarine fighter. Even prior to its 'finest hour', Hurricanes provided the first RAF aces of the war in France during the *Blitzkrieg*. In 1940/41 the Mark I saw action in the Mediterranean and East and North Africa, fighting valiantly against numerically superior Italian forces. Finally, in 1942, a veritable handful of tropicalised Hurricane Is attempted to halt the Japanese invasion of the Far East, the fighter seeing action over Singapore, Malaya, Burma and Java. Although the last Mk I was built in 1941, later Hurricane variants remained in production until September 1944.

Hurricane Mk I P2921/'GZ-L' of Flt Lt 'Pete' Brothers, No 32 Sqn, Biggin Hill/Hawkinge, July 1940

This Hurricane was one of three Hawker fighters sent to No 32 Sqn on 11 June 1940 as attrition replacements for the trio of aircraft lost by the unit in combat during a patrol over Le Tréport 48 hours earlier. As the newest of the three to arrive at Biggin Hill, P2921 was immediately 'acquired' by 'B' Flight commander, 'Pete' Brothers. He flew P2921 throughout July and August 1940, during which time he was credited

with destroying eight German aircraft (six Bf 109Es, a Bf 110 and a Do 17). The fighter remained with No 32 Sqn until 21 February 1941, when it was transferred to the newly-formed No 315 'Polish' Sqn at Speke, near Liverpool.

BLUNTING OF THE ZERSTÖRER

'Christ! It's worse than a Hendon air pageant. A horde of dots are filling the sky; below us bombers flying in close formation – Ju 88s and 87s. Above them, towering tier above tier, are fighters – 110s and 109s.'

Hauptmann Eric Groth and Oberleutnant Hans-Joachim Jabs pose for an official photo in front of a II./ZG 76 Bf 110C at Jever soon after they had each been presented with the Knight's Cross on 1 October 1940. Groth was Jabs' *Gruppenkommandeur*, and had scored 12 kills up to this point in the war – Jabs was the leading *Zerstörer* ace at the time with 19 victories. Eric Groth survived until 11 August 1941, when he was killed in a Bf 110 crash near Stavanger, in Norway, whilst flying on instruments in bad weather (*Hans-Joachim Jabs via Peter Hinchliffe*)

15 August 1940 – the height of the Battle of Britain. And early evening over the Hampshire coast as Hans-Joachim Jabs of 6./ZG 76 points the Sharksmouth nose of his Bf 110C 'Nordpol-Paula' back out over the Channel to escape the attentions of a pair of prowling No 87 Sqn Hurricanes up from Exeter. Tasked with escorting a formation of Ju 88 bombers attacking Worthy Down and Middle Wallop, II./ZG 76 and their charges had been met by no fewer than eight squadrons of RAF fighters. Jabs' claiming two Spitfires and a Hurricane was little recompense for the grievous losses suffered by the 'Sharksmouths' during the ensuing action. Altogether, Major Erich Groth's *Gruppe* lost eight Bf 110s, with a total of 14 aircrew reported killed, missing or wounded on this day.

Two of the Bf 110s downed during this hard fought engagement fell to No 87 Sqn Hurricane ace Flt Lt Ian 'Widge'

Gleed, who recounted the action from the British perspective in his excellent wartime autobiography *Arise to Conquer*;

"'Hell! There they are". I speak on the R.T. "Hullo, Suncup Leader. Tally-ho! Bandits just to our right. Line astern, line astern, go". I slam my glasshouse shut. "Christ! It's worse than a Hendon air pageant". A horde of dots are filling the sky; below us bombers flying in close formation – Ju 88s and 87s. Above them, towering tier above tier, are fighters – 110s and 109s. The mass comes closer.

"Now steady; don't go in too soon – work round into the sun". The bombers pass about 10,000 ft below us. I start a dive, craning my neck to see behind. A circle of 110s are just in front of us; they turn in a big circle. Suddenly, the white of the crosses on their wings jumps into shape. I kick on the rudder; my sights are just in front of one. "Get the right deflection". Now I press the firing-button – a terrific burst of orange flame; it seems to light the whole sky. Everything goes grey as I bank into a turn. "Ease off a bit, you fool, or you'll spin". I push the stick forward – white puffs flash past my cockpit. "Blast you, rear-gunners!" I climb steeply, turning hard. Just above me there is another circle of 110s; their bellies are pale blue, looking very clean.

'"Look out! Look out" Oh God! A Hurricane just in front of me is shooting at a 110; another 110 is on its tail. Hell! It's too far for me to reach. The 110 goes vertically downwards followed by the Hurricane – "Hell, you bastards!" A stream of tracer from behind just misses my right wing. I turn hard to the left; two splashes appear in the calm sea; already it is dotted with oily patches. For a second I get my sights on another 110. He turns and gives me an easy deflection shot. I thumb the trigger; a puff of white smoke comes from his engine. Almost lazily he turns on his back and starts an inverted, over the vertical, dive. I steep turn.

Down, down he goes – a white splash. At the same time two other splashes and a cloud of smoke go up from the beach. Four 'planes have hit the deck within a second.'

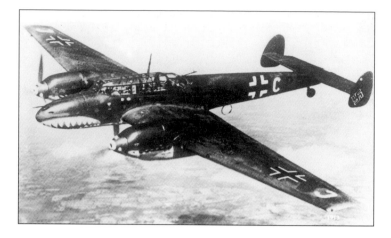

Undoubtedly the most widely recognised *Zerstörer* 'badge' of the period was II./ZG 76's fearsome 'Sharksmouth'. 'M8+CP', pictured here, was a 6. *Staffel* machine (*via John Weal*)

Having survived the carnage wrought on the *Zerstörergeschwader* during the summer of 1940, Oberleutnant Jabs can indeed afford to flash a smile at the camera prior to climbing aboard his 'sharksmouthed' II./ZG 76 Bf 110C, which already has its engines running. The snowy ground below the heavy fighter indicates that winter has arrived at Jever (*via John Weal*)

PILOT BIOGRAPHY – HANS-JOACHIM JABS

Hans-Joachim Jabs was one of the relatively few Luftwaffe combat pilots to fight throughout the war from beginning to end. In his case, this feat was all the more remarkable because his mount was the twin-engined Bf 110 day *Zerstörer* (and later nightfighter), which was a machine regarded by almost every Allied aircraft that encountered it – with the exception of unarmed trainers – as 'easy pickings'.

Originally trained as a Bf 109 pilot, Jabs transferred to II./ZG 76 (the famous 'Sharksmouth' *Gruppe*) in March 1940, arriving just in time to participate in the Battle of France. By the end of that campaign he was already an ace, having downed four French fighters and two RAF Spitfires.

In the Battle of Britain which followed, the myth of the *Zerstörer*, or heavy fighter, was effectively shattered. The *Zerstörer* arm was decimated over southern England, never fully to recover. But unlike many of his comrades, Hans-Joachim Jabs not only survived, he actually continued to score, adding eight more Spitfires and four more Hurricanes to his total by the time the Battle reached its climax in mid September. This feat was recognised by the award of the Knight's Cross to Oberleutnant Jabs on 1 October 1940 when his score was standing at 19 enemy aircraft destroyed. One more would be added to this tally before Jabs, together with the bulk of the remaining day *Zerstörer*, was remustered into the burgeoning nightfighting force.

Rising to the rank of oberleutnant, and the command of NJG 1, by war's end Jabs had achieved 28 victories by night. But old habits apparently die hard, for on 29 April 1944 he claimed a brace of Spitfire Mk IXs over his Arnhem-Deelen base in broad daylight!

Hans-Joachim Jabs, who celebrates his 83rd birthday in November 2000, lives in Lüdenscheid, in Germany, where he still runs a prosperous business selling heavy agricultural machinery.

SPECIFICATION

Messerschmitt Bf 110C
(all dimensions and performance data for Bf 110C-4 fighter-destroyer variant)

TYPE:	twin-engined monoplane fighter
ACCOMMODATION:	two-/three-man crew
DIMENSIONS:	length 39 ft 8.5 in (12.10 m)
	wingspan 53 ft 4.75 in (16.27 m)
	height 11 ft 6 in (3.50 m)
WEIGHTS:	empty 9920 lb (4500 kg)
	normal loaded 15,300 lb (6940 kg)
PERFORMANCE:	maximum speed 349 mph (561 kmh)
	range 565 miles (909 km)
	powerplants two Daimler-Benz DB 601A-1 engines
	output 2200 hp (1640 kW)
ARMAMENT:	two 20 mm cannon and four 7.9 mm machine guns in nose cowling, 7.9 mm machine gun in rear cockpit
FIRST FLIGHT DATE:	late 1938
OPERATORS:	Germany
PRODUCTION:	approximately 6050 (all models)

Designed in 1934-35 to fill the perceived need for a high-speed, long-range, heavily-armed twin-engined fighter, Messerschmitt's Bf 110 *Zerstörer* (destroyer) fulfilled all these criterion. Seen as the ultimate bomber escort, capable of sweeping the sky clean of enemy fighters, the Bf 110 relied more on its firepower than manoeuvrability to survive in combat. Too late to see action in the Spanish Civil War, the Bf 110C made the aircraft's combat debut over Poland, where it dominated the skies in an environment of overwhelming Luftwaffe air superiority. These successes continued throughout the 'Phoney War' and into the early days of the *Blitzkrieg* in the west, but come the Battle of Britain, serious flaws in the *Zerstörer* concept were cruelly exposed. Indeed, by the latter stages of this epic aerial conflict between the RAF and the Luftwaffe, the 'destroyer' was only allowed to venture across the Channel when its own dedicated single-seat fighter escort was available! Following the loss of over 200 Bf 110s during the campaign, the day fighter role was given over almost exclusively to the single-seat Bf 109E *gruppe*, and the Messerschmitt 'twin' sent to operate on less hostile fronts in the Balkans and the Mediterranean.

The 'Sharksmouths'' four leading *Experten*, and all future Knight's Cross holders. They are from left to right, Oberleutnants Hans-Joachim Jabs and Wilhelm Herget (both of 6./ZG 76), Hauptmann Erich Groth (*Gruppenkommandeur* II./ZG 76) and Hauptmann Heinz Nacke (*Staffelkapitän* 6./ZG 76) (*via John Weal*)

Bf 110C 'M8+NP' of Oberleutnant Hans-Joachim Jabs, 6./ZG 76, France, May 1940
Wearing standard early war camouflage (schwarzgrün 70/dunkelgrün 71 upper surfaces and hellblau 65 undersides) and a textbook set of national insignia of the period, this aircraft also boasts arguably the most famous, and certainly the best known, Bf 110 unit marking of them all – II./ZG 76's distinctive 'Sharksmouth'. Representative of the *gruppe* at the height of its power, Jabs' machine is depicted during ZG 76's headlong advance across France in the late spring/early summer of 1940. His first six kills are already displayed on the tailfin of the big 'fighter-destroyer'.

BATTLE OF BRITAIN DAY

'Literally thousands of yellow-nosed Messerschmitts were whistling by all around me less than 100 yards away, so I pulled the bloody stick back, went into a steep turn, and held it there!'

Sgt George 'Grumpy' Unwin and Flash, his Alsation, pose by chocked No 19 Sqn Spitfire I K9798 at Duxford in late 1938 (*George Unwin*)

'I was lucky to survive that second sortie unscathed, as through my own stupidity I got separated from the rest of the Wing. We were led through a gap in the cloud over London by Sqn Ldr Bader of No 242 Sqn, and there in front of us was a sight that looked just like a pre-war Hendon air pageant flypast. We were at about 23,000 ft and the bombers were below us at 20,000. In my familiar position as Red Three in Sqn Ldr "Sandy" Lane's leading section, I was transfixed by a squadron of Hurricanes struggling to engage the bombers below us – so much so that I had completely forgotten about their escort, and subsequently flew straight into the middle of them! The next thing I knew, literally thousands of yellow-nosed Messerschmitts were whistling by all around me less than 100 yards away, so I pulled the bloody stick back, went into a steep turn, and held it there!

'I gave the odd machine a quick burst as it flew past me, and succeeded in forcing one to half roll and dive into cloud below. I followed him down, but my windscreen froze at 6000 ft and he escaped. I then climbed back up to 25,000 ft in search of my wingmates, but as was often the case in these aerial duels, the sky had gone from being heavy with aircraft to totally empty in a

matter of seconds. After several minutes I spotted a pair of Bf 109s above me, flying back in a loose 'rotte' formation towards the Channel, obviously intent on heading home. After a long chase, I finally caught them as they crossed the Kent coast at Lydd, and after firing a long burst into the trailing fighter, it immediately burst into flames and crashed just offshore. Inexplicably, the leader failed to take any evasive action following the demise of his wingman, and he too was shot down on fire into the sea seconds later. I then flew back to Fowlmere alone.

'I had survived this mission simply because the Spitfire could sustain a continuous rate of turn inside the Bf 109E without stalling – the latter was known for flicking into a vicious stall spin without prior warning if pulled around too tightly. The Spitfire would give a shudder to signal it was close to the edge, so as soon as you felt the shake you eased off the stick pressure.

'We were always on the defensive during 1940 due to the ceiling advantage enjoyed by the enemy. Our staple tactic to counter this was to turn straight into them so that they couldn't latch onto your tail. You then pulled on the "g" in the hope that your own superior rate of turn would allow you to whip around on their tails. Often, having performed this manoeuvre on two or three consecutive occasions, you would right yourself only to find the sky empty of friend and foe! Then the search began all over again.'

No 19 Sqn's Sgt Bernard Jennings scrambles from Fowlmere (Duxford's satellite station during World War 2) in Spitfire IA X4474 as part of George Unwin's Yellow Section during the height of the Battle of Britain. On Friday, 27 September 1940, this combat pairing were credited with the destruction of a Bf 109E from JG 54 during a huge dogfight south of the Thames that saw No 19 Sqn pilots claim a further seven *Emils* destroyed (*via Jerry Scutts*)

Yet another Channel sweep safely completed, a battle-seasoned Flt Sgt George Unwin climbs out of his Spitfire I K9853 at Fowlmere in late June 1940. To the left of his flying boot is a rare piece of early-war nose art in the form of a 'Popeye' figure about to deliver his famous 'Twisker Sock' punch. A member of George's groundcrew had painted this cartoon figure on K9853 several weeks prior to No 19 Sqn going into combat over France in late May. During this period Unwin flew several different Spitfires on combat patrols across the Channel, although this particular machine, coded 'QV-H', was his favourite. Indeed, he claimed a He 111 probable whilst flying K9853 over Dunkirk on his second patrol of 1 June. Earlier that same day he had used K9856 to down a Bf 110 whilst defending the evacuation beaches, plus claim a second *Zerstörer* as a probable. 'QV-H' had been with the squadron since 31 January 1939, first being flown by Unwin on 15 March that same year. After serving with the unit for almost 18 months, it was sent to General Aircraft Limited for overhaul on 15 July 1940 following No 19 Sqn's re-equipment with the less than successful cannon-armed Mk IB. K9853 was then issued to Training Command, and was written off in a heavy landing before the end of September (*George Unwin*)

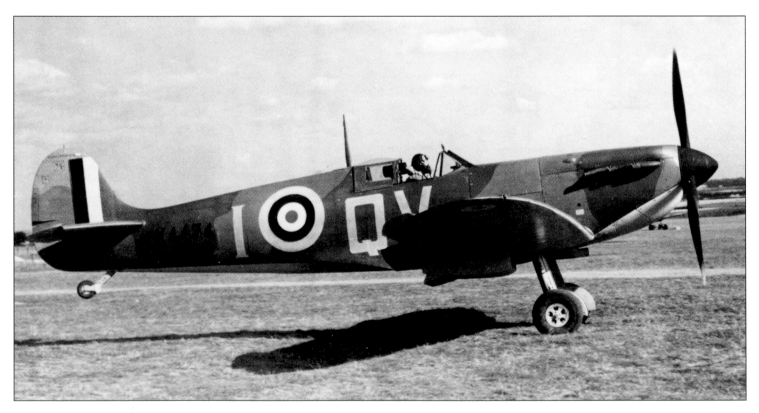

X4474 has its guns hurriedly tended at Fowlmere by Airman Fred Roberts in late September 1940, in anticipation of its next scramble. Already strapped into the cockpit, Sgt Jennings converses with his rigger about rectification work carried out on the fighter since its last flight (*via Jerry Scutts*)

SPECIFICATION

Supermarine Spitfire Mk I/II
(all dimensions and performance data for Spitfire Mk IA)

TYPE:	single-engined monoplane fighter
ACCOMMODATION:	pilot
DIMENSIONS:	length 29 ft 11 in (9.12 m) wingspan 36 ft 10 in (11.23 m) height 11 ft 5 in (3.48 m)
WEIGHTS:	empty 4810 lb (2182 kg) loaded weight 5844 lb (2651 kg)
PERFORMANCE:	maximum speed 355 mph (571 kmh) range 575 miles (925 km) powerplant Rolls-Royce Merlin II/III output 1030 hp (768 kW)
ARMAMENT:	eight 0.303 in machine guns in wings
FIRST FLIGHT DATE:	5 March 1936
OPERATORS:	Australia, Canada, New Zealand, UK
PRODUCTION:	1567 Mk Is and 921 Mk IIs

The only British fighter to remain in production throughout World War 2, the exploits of the Supermarine Spitfire are legendary. Over 20,000 were produced in mark numbers ranging from I through to 24, this total also including over 1000 built as dedicated Seafire fleet fighters for the Royal Navy. Designed by Reginald J Mitchell following his experiences with the RAF's Schneider Trophy winning Supermarine floatplanes of the 1920s and 30s, prototype Spitfire K5054 first took to the skies on 6 March 1936, powered by the soon to be equally famous Rolls-Royce Merlin I engine. However, due to production problems encountered with the revolutionary stressed-skin construction of the fighter, it was to be another two-and-a-half years before the first examples entered service with Fighter Command. Spitfire Mk Is and IIs served only briefly in frontline squadrons with the RAF (exclusively on the Channel Front) once the war had started, but their pilots were responsible for achieving impressive scores against the all-conquering Luftwaffe during the Battles of France and Britain. Although early-mark Spitfires were notorious for their light armament, overheating engines due to inadequate cooling and short range, many of the pilots that flew the Mk Is and IIs regarded the first production machines as the best handling of the breed, being a 'true aviator's aircraft' due to its excellent power-to-weight ratio and beautifully harmonised flying controls.

PILOT BIOGRAPHY – GEORGE 'GRUMPY' UNWIN

A member of No 19 Sqn from 1936, and one of the RAF's most experienced Spitfire service pilots at the outbreak of war, Flt Sgt George 'Grumpy' Unwin was the unit's senior NCO throughout the long summer of 1940. First engaging the enemy over the evacuation beaches of Dunkirk during Operation *Dynamo*, he was later awarded the Distinguished Flying Medal (DFM) and Bar for his successful participation in both this action and the Battle of Britain. By the time he was posted away from the unit at the end of 1940, having been deemed too old at 28 by Fighter Command to serve within its frontline force, Unwin had been credited with 13 and 2 shared aircraft confirmed destroyed, two unconfirmed victories and a solitary damaged claim. These successes made him No 19 Sqn's leading ace of 1940.

Today, George 'Grumpy' Unwin lives quietly in Dorset, his modest abode backing onto a golf course on which he plays a round virtually every day. His RAF career spanned three decades across the globe, and he eventually attained the rank of wing commander. However, he categorically states that his two-and-a-half year spell as an NCO on Spitfires (during which time he flew no less than 48 different aircraft) with No 19 Sqn at Duxford was the pinnacle of his career as a fighter pilot.

Spitfire Mk IB R6776/'QV-H' of Flt Sgt George Unwin, No 19 Sqn, Fowlmere, August/ September 1940

This aircraft was one of the original cannon-armed Spitfire IBs issued to No 19 Sqn for a brief period in the summer of 1940. Unlike the majority of the unit's pilots, who struggled with the reliability of the twin cannon armament in their Mk IBs, Unwin enjoyed some success in this aircraft, claiming a Bf 110 destroyed and another probably destroyed on 16

August, followed by a third Bf 110 confirmed destroyed on 3 September. Later, the aircraft was modified into a Mk VB, and went on to serve with Nos 92, 316 and 306 Sqns, before being written off in May 1942 after sustaining Category E battle damage during a sweep over France.

FINAL VICTORY

'I was Yellow 3 and was weaving merrily behind, keeping an eagle eye above, when I caught a glimpse of three "yellow noses" in my mirror. They were obviously crack pilots by their tight formation and strategy.'

The Luftwaffe's most successful fighter pilot during the latter half of 1940, Oberleutnant Helmut Wick of JG 2 gained the Knight's Cross for 20 victories on 27 August and was featured on the front page of a Berlin weekly magazine the following month. By then his score was already passed the 22-mark depicted on the tail of his Bf 109E, which 'snuck' into the corner of this carefully posed propaganda shot (*via John Weal*)

Sensing that his 56th kill is just moments away, then ranking *Jagdwaffe* ace Major Helmut Wick turns in behind the already smoking Spitfire I (R6631) of No 609 'West Riding' Sqn's Plt Off Paul A Baillon as the pair race over The Needles at the western end of the Isle of Wight on the afternoon of 28 November 1940. Having used his height advantage to power-dive into the auxiliary squadron as it patrolled over the Solent, the newly-promoted *Geschwaderkommodore* of JG 2 'Richthofen' had quickly singled out the hapless Baillon and hit his Spitfire hard with a well aimed burst of fire from Bf 109E-4 Wk-Nr 5344 – Wick's favoured mount throughout late 1940.

Canadian ace Plt Off Keith A Ogilvie was part of the No 609 Sqn formation engaged by I./JG 2, and he described the attack in the following terms;

'I was Yellow 3 and was weaving merrily behind, keeping an eagle eye above, when I caught a glimpse of three "yellow noses" in my mirror. They were obviously crack pilots by their tight formation and strategy. I gave the warning and dove as the centre

"Johnny" opened fire on me, and was speeded on my way by a cannon shot up the fuselage and a second through my prop.'

Despite having had his aircraft superficially damaged in the initial attack, Ogilvie shook off his assailants and saw Plt Off Baillon bail out of his stricken Spitfire about 20 miles south of Bournemouth. He followed his squadronmate's progress down into the water, but was dismayed to see the pilot display no signs of life whilst floating beneath the perfectly deployed parachute. Baillon's body was later washed up on the Normandy coast.

His conqueror, meanwhile, had little time to celebrate his latest kill, for whilst recovering from the dive Wick banked steeply, and for a split-second flashed across the nose of another Spitfire. Instinctively, its pilot, either Flt Lt John 'Cocky' Dundas DFC of No 609 Sqn (the unit's leading ace with 16 kills) in Spitfire I X4586, or veteran Pole Sgt Zygmunt Klein, flying Spitfire I P9427 of No 152 Sqn, opened fire. The short burst must have mortally damaged the heavily mottled Messerschmitt, for Wick jettisoned his canopy and jumped over the side. The solitary parachute

drifting down towards the sea south-west of The Needles would be the last anybody ever saw of the Luftwaffe's leading ace, for an intensive air and sea searches failed to find Wick.

The *Kommodore* shared his watery grave with his victor, who was downed just minutes later by Wick's distraught wingman, 'Rudi' Pflanz. Confirmation of just who shot the great ace down remains a mystery to this day, as both Dundas and Klein failed to return from the sortie.

Ironically, the *Jagdwaffe's* then leading ace was not supposed to be over the Isle of Wight at all on this fateful day, for a signal had arrived at the *Geschwader's* HQ at Beaumont-le-Roger prohibiting him from all further combat flying. However, this was received minutes after Wick had taken off with his *Stabsschwarm* on what would ultimately prove to be his final fighter sweep of his favourite hunting ground over the Channel to the south of the Solent.

ABOVE By the end of October 1940 the cult of the 'fighter ace' had taken firm hold in the German Homeland. This magazine page is devoted to eight of the early Knight's Cross winners, and is headed 'Not one of them over 30 years of age' (*via John Weal*)

ABOVE RIGHT Two final ironies surround Helmut Wicks' loss. Moments after he had taken off on his final flight, an order was received at *Geschwader* HQ prohibiting him from all further combat flying. He was now considered too valuable to risk, and henceforth was to use his remarkable skills in training new pilots. Also, he once again adorned the cover of Berlin's best-selling weekly. Here, he is seen on the far right of the picture, which carried the caption 'The *Reichsmarschall* visits the *Jagdgeschwader* Richthofen'- and the date of Issue No 48, top left . . . 28 November 1940! (*via John Weal*)

RIGHT Unlike many other *Jagdflieger*, Helmut Wick retained the same aircraft throughout most of the latter part of his brief, but illustrious, career. Here, his Bf 109E-4 Wk-Nr 5344, seen on the flattened wheat that was Beaumont-le-Roger throughout the Battle of Britain, sports *Gruppenkommandeur's* chevrons. Note also the *Staffel* badge for 3./JG 2 on the cowling, the *Geschwader* badge beneath the windscreen, the unusual presentation of the fuselage cross and the kill bars on the rudder. The whitewalled tailwheel tyre also adds a nice touch (*via John Weal*)

PILOT BIOGRAPHY – HELMUT WICK

The meteoric rise of Helmut Wick – from a *Rottenfuhrer* (leader of a two-aircraft formation) to *Geschwaderkommodore* of JG 2 'Richthofen', the Luftwaffe's premier fighter unit – was unparalleled in the annals of that service's history.

As a 24-year-old leutnant, it was Wick who scored JG 2's first victory of World War 2 when he downed a French Curtiss Hawk on 22 November 1939 during the period of the so-called 'Phoney War'. He did not add to his own tally until the *Blitzkrieg* in the west was well underway, claiming a trio of LeO 451 bombers on 17 May 1940. But in the six months which followed, a steady succession of victories would make Wick the most successful fighter pilot of the entire Luftwaffe.

He emerged from the Battle of France with 14 kills (plus two unconfirmed), and in July 1940 he was appointed *Staffelkapitän* of 3./JG 2. It was during the Battle of Britain that his dual qualities of marksmanship and leadership really came to the fore. A lengthening list of successes earned Wick awards, promotion and the adulation of the German press, and on 27 August, as an oberleutnant, he received the Knight's Cross for 20 victories. He became *Gruppenkommandeur* of I./JG 2 the following month, and was awarded the Oak Leaves on 6 October – by which time his score had risen to 42.

Already a major, Wick was given command of JG 2 'Richthofen' exactly a fortnight later. But fate was soon to overtake him. On 28 November, the Luftwaffe's then ranking ace with 56 kills was himself shot down south of the Isle of Wight. Although he parachuted into the English Channel, not trace of Helmut Wick was ever found.

SPECIFICATION

Messerschmitt Bf 109E
(all dimensions and performance data for Bf 109E-3)

TYPE:	single-engined monoplane fighter
ACCOMMODATION:	pilot
DIMENSIONS:	length 28 ft 0 in (8.55 m) wingspan 32 ft 4.5 in (0.07 m) height 8 ft 2 in (2.49 m)
WEIGHTS:	empty 4189 lb (1900 kg) maximum take-off 5875 lb (2665 kg)
PERFORMANCE:	maximum speed 348 mph (560 kmh) range 410 miles (660 km) powerplant Daimler-Benz DB 601Aa output 1175 hp (876 kW)
ARMAMENT:	two 7.9 mm machine guns in upper cowling, two 20 mm cannon in wings; some E-3s had additional 20 mm cannon in propeller hub; fighter-bomber (250-kg) bomb under fuselage
FIRST FLIGHT DATE:	June 1937 (Bf 109 V10)
OPERATORS:	Bulgaria, Croatia, Germany, Romania, Slovakia, Spain, Switzerland, Yugoslavia
PRODUCTION:	approximately 4000

Designed to meet a 1934 *Reichluftfahrtministerium* (RLM) requirement for a single-seat monoplane fighter, the original Bf 109 V1 was the winning competitor in a 'fly off' that involved three other designs from proven German aviation companies. Light and small, the first production-standard Bf 109s (B-1 models) to enter service in early 1937 proved their worth during the Spanish Civil War. By the time Germany invaded Poland in September 1939, the re-engined Bf 109E was rolling off the Messerschmitt production line in great quantity, the now-familiar airframe being paired up with the powerful Daimler-Benz DB 601. This combination had been tested as long ago as June 1937, when a pre-production aircraft had been flown with a carburetted DB 600 fitted in place of the D-model's Junkers Jumo 210Da, but the subsequent availability of the Bf 109E had been hampered by delays in the development of the appreciably more powerful Daimler-Benz engine. However, these problems had been sorted out by early 1939. Built in huge numbers, and in a great array of sub-variants for the fighter, reconnaissance, fighter-bomber and shipboard fighter roles, the Bf 109E proved to be the master of all its European contemporaries bar the Spitfire Mk I/II, to which it was considered an equal. Aside from fighting over Poland, the E-model saw combat throughout the *Blitzkrieg* of 1940 and the Battle of Britain which followed, in the Balkans in 1941 and in the opening phases of the North African and Soviet campaigns.

Bf 109E-4 (Wk-Nr 5344) 'Black Double Chevron' of Hauptmann Helmut Wick,
***Gruppenkommandeur* of I./JG 2 'Richthofen', Beaumont-le-Roger, October 1940**
Depicted midway in its evolution from 'Yellow 2' to full *Kommodore's* markings, Wk-Nr 5344 is shown in profile soon after it had received its coat of very close dapple overall. Note also the 'toning down' of the fuselage cross by reducing the white areas, and the pale yellow cowling (thin yellow wash over white). Certain inconsistencies in the presentation and grouping of the victory bars point to 5344's having had a number of replacement rudders during its career. The 'Richthofen' *Geschwader* badge is carried beneath the windscreen, while that on the cowling (long thought to be Wick's personal emblem) is the insignia of 3./JG 2, designed some time earlier by a *Staffel* member who chose the colours blue and yellow in honour of the then *Kapitän* Hennig Strümpell's Swedish ancestry.

North African Hawk

'They seemed far keener to collaborate with the Germans, opposing our efforts with rather more enthusiasm and courage than they had shown when trying to defend their country from invasion in 1940.'

Georges Lemare is seen strapped into a 4th *Escadrille* 'Caen' Normandie-Niémen Yak-3 in early 1945, having at last achieved ace status (*via Barry Ketley*)

In order to protect Allied shipping from the growing U-boat menace off the west coast of Africa and south of Gibraltar, the RAF established a permanent base at Bathurst, in Gambia, in January 1941. To protect these increasingly vulnerable convoys, detachments of Sunderland I flying boats were spread along the west coast. As more aircraft arrived, so Bathurst became the 'hub' for these operations in West Africa. One of those units posted into the theatre was No 204 Sqn, which moved from the Icelandic capital, Reykjavik, to Bathurst on 28 August.

Ironically, the greatest threat faced by the Sunderland crews in West Africa was not posed by German fighters, but rather Vichy French aircraft based in the neighbouring colonies of French West Africa (now Senegal). One such unit was GC I/4, which had seen much action during the Battle for France the previous year, before

retreating to North Africa following the French surrender in late June. Equipped with Curtiss H-75 Hawks, the unit was manned by seasoned fighter pilots who had scored numerous kills in the ill-fated defence of their country. One such individual was *Sergent Chef* Georges Lemare, who had claimed his first victory as long ago as 13 January 1940, and his most recent on 24 September 1940 whilst opposing attacks on Dakar by aircraft launched from HMS *Ark Royal*.

By late September 1941 the Sunderlands were encountering Vichy French fighters on virtually all of their long-range patrols over coastal convoys in the area. As the month progressed, so the

Iain Wyllie

Hawk pilots became more aggressive in their attempts to keep the skies of Dakar clear of RAF aircraft. Indeed, one Sunderland aircrewman stated that 'they seemed far keener to collaborate with the Germans, opposing our efforts with rather more enthusiasm and courage than they had shown when trying to defend their country from invasion in 1940'.

Things finally came to a head on 29 September when two Sunderlands from No 204 Sqn were attacked by French Hawks directly off the coast of Dakar. Flying H-75 s/n 295 was Sgt Lemare, who made several passes at N9044/KG-C until he broke off his attack following accurate defensive fire from the Sunderland. The flying boat was left with its 'third pilot' dead and smoke streaming from a knocked out engine. Once back at GC I/4's base at Dakar-Oukam, Lemare was awarded a 'damaged', which proved an accurate assessment, for N9044 limped back south to Bathurst on three engines, and was later repaired and returned to service.

Georges Lemare would have to wait a further three years to finally 'make ace', shooting down an Fw 190 on 20 October 1944 while flying a Yak-3 with the *Normandie-Niémen* on the Russian Front. Having seen action on three fronts, and fought both for and against the Allies, Lemare would survive the war with a total of 13 kills to his credit.

Sgt Georges Lemare of 2e *Escadrille* of GC I/4 was photographed in his H-75A-3 No 295 whilst on a patrol from Cap-Vert, near Dakar. His aircraft wears full Vichy markings from the 1941-42 period. At this time he had four victories to his name, and the rest of his tally would be amassed whilst flying with the *Normandie-Niémen* in Russia (*via Barry Ketley*)

Lemare breaks away from the camera in his GC I/4 Hawk during the patrol. This aircraft had previously been used by the unit in France during the German invasion of 1940 (*via Barry Ketley*)

PILOT BIOGRAPHY – GEORGES LEMARE

Born on 16 November 1917 in Barenton, Normandy, Georges Lemare began his military training at Versailles in April 1937, where he chose to become a pilot. Transferred to the flying school at Bourges in May, he showed early promise by gaining his pilot's brevet two months later. In January 1938 he was posted to the 2nd *Escadrille* of GC I/4.

Aware of the imminence of war, the commander of the unit drove his men hard in training. The adjutant at the time was Louis Delfino, with whom Lemare was later to serve in Russia. By August 1939, GC I/4 was based at Wez-Thuisy, from where Lemare took part in many patrols tasked with aerial defence of the numerous French airfields in the area. The 'Phoney War', however, ensured that Lemare saw no action until November. By then GC I/4 was operating from Norrent-Fontes, and it was from there, in the appalling weather of January 1940, while flying a Hawk, that he first encountered the Luftwaffe when he shared a Do 17 with Capitaine Barbier. His next confirmed victory was not until 20 May when he shot down a Ju 88 which was attacking a large vessel off the beach at Dunkirk. A Bf 109 followed near Picquigny on 6 June.

By 10 June 1940 (the day of the French collapse) Lemare had retreated with his unit to Meknes, in Morocco, before moving to Dakar in French West Africa on 16 July. By now part of the Vichy French air force, Lemare's next claim was a Fleet Air Arm Swordfish over Dakar on 24 September. Despite many subsequent patrols, Lemare saw little action until he intercepted a No 204 Sqn Sunderlands off the coast on 29 September 1941.

Four months after he was posted back to France in July 1942, the Germans occupied the whole of the country following the Allied landings in North Africa. At this point Lemare decided to make his escape. He eventually reached Spain in January 1943, and was eventually repatriated to North Africa in August, where he rejoined his old unit, but this time on the side of the Allies. Given the job of coastal patrols, Lemare and Louis Delfino quickly decided that the *Normandie-Niémen* offered more opportunities for combat. Consquently they embarked for Russia in January 1944. Arriving in March, Lemare soon found himself posted to the 4th *Escadrille* 'Caen'.

Flying Yak fighters, Lemare shot down three Fw 190s and three Bf 109s during a single week (20-27 October 1944) over East Prussia. The following spring, during the next major Soviet offensive against East Prussia, he added two more Fw 190s destroyed and a third damaged. His last kill was a Bf 109 on 27 March 1945 to bring his official list of confirmed victories to 13 confirmed and 2 damaged.

After returning to France, he began a career in civil aviation but was killed when his Bloch 161 crashed near Romanville on 28 January 1948.

Hawk H75A-3 '9' (s/n 295) of Sgt Georges Lemare, 2e *Escadrille* of GC I/4, Dakar-Oukam, September 1941

This aircraft has had its standard 1940-style European camouflage modified 'in the field' to suit North African conditions through the overpainting of the grey sections of its upper camouflage with sand-coloured paint. Not visible in this view is a repeat of the black disc and number on the lower lip of the engine cowling.

SPECIFICATION

Curtiss P-36/Hawk H-75

TYPE:	single-engined monoplane fighter
ACCOMMODATION:	pilot
DIMENSIONS:	length 28 ft 6 in (8.69 m)
	wingspan 37 ft 3.5 in (11.37 m)
	height 12 ft 2 in (3.71 m)
WEIGHTS:	empty 4567 lb (2072 kg)
	maximum take-off 6010 lb (2726 kg)
PERFORMANCE:	maximum speed 300 mph (483 kmh)
	range 825 miles (1328 km)
	powerplant Pratt & Whitney R-1830-13 Twin Wasp
	output 1050 hp (783 kW)
ARMAMENT:	one 0.30 in and one 0.50 in machine gun in nose, with additional two 0.30 in machine guns in wings; French Hawk H-75A had up to six machine guns, and provision for 400 lb (181 kg) of underwing bombs
FIRST FLIGHT DATE:	15 May 1935 (Model 75) and February 1937 (Y1P-36)
OPERATORS:	Argentina, China, Finland, France, The Netherlands East Indies, Norway, Peru, Portugal, South Africa, Thailand, UK, USA
PRODUCTION:	1424

Forerunner of the famous Hawk series of fighters produced in great numbers by Curtiss during World War 2, the original Model 75 was the losing design in a competition fly-off held by the US Army Air Corps (USAAC) for a new monoplane fighter in mid-1935. Beaten by the Seversky P-35, the Curtiss design was overhauled by the company primarily through the fitment of a more powerful Twin Wasp engine. The resulting Y1P-36 was ordered into production in 1936, and by the time of the Pearl Harbor raid on 7 December 1941, some 209 P-36A/Cs had been delivered to the USAAC. Export orders were also received by Curtiss for their fighter, which was designated the Hawk 75 by the company when built for foreign use. Large numbers were received by a clutch of nations, including around 350 (out of an order for 620) by the French, which were subsequently credited with destroying 311 German aircraft during the Battle of France. Those H-75As that survived the collapse of France were sent to French colonial territories in North and West Africa in mid-1940, where they formed the backbone of the Vichy French air force until the *Torch* invasion of late 1942. Other Hawk 75s not delivered to France prior to the *Blitzkrieg* were issued instead to the RAF (who called them Mohawk Is), and they subsequently saw action in the Far East against the Japanese in 1942-43.

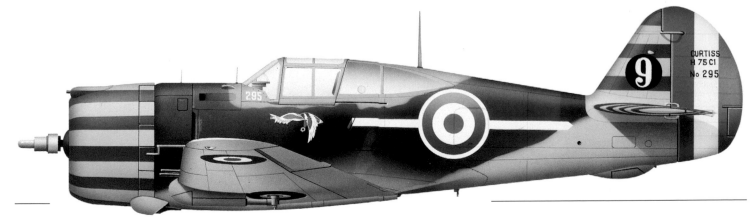

'STAR OF AFRIKA'

'In combat I make all my motions unconsciously. This lets me concentrate fully on the attack, and fly my plane as though I had wings.'

'All the enemy aircraft were shot down by Marseille that day in a turning dogfight. He displayed an unmistakable talent for deflection shooting. As soon as he shot, he needed only to glance at the enemy plane. His pattern began at the front, at the engine's nose, and consistently ended in the cockpit.

'How he was able to do this, hitting his mark so precisely in a hundredth of a second, he himself couldn't even explain, and as a result, can't relay his secret to his comrades at arms.

'With every dogfight, however, I was able to notice that during a turning duel he would throttle his plane's speed back as far as possible. This enabled him to fly a tighter turn and be a bit lower than his opponent. Then, with a sudden burst of fire, the enemy would be splattered across the sky. His ammunition expenditure in this dramatic air battle came to a total of 360 rounds.'

This report was lodged by Unteroffizier Rainer Pöttgen, who served as wingman (*Rottenflieger*) to the Luftwaffe's most successful fighter ace in North Africa, Hans-Joachim 'Jochen' Marseille. It refers to an eleven-minute dogfight that took place in the early afternoon of 3 June 1942 between six Bf 109F-4/Z Trops from 3./JG 27 and nine Tomahawk Is from No 5 Sqn, South African Air Force. The German fighters were protecting Ju 87 Stukas from I./StG 3 that had been sent to bomb the beleaguered French fort at Bir Hachiem, south-east of Tobruk.

'Jochen' Marseille, wearing a favourite leather flying jacket, acknowledges the photographer as his 50th victory is recorded on the rudder of his first Bf 109F-4/Z Trop, Wk-Nr 12593. The rows of kills were easily applied with the aid of the stencil held by the groundcrewman in his left hand. Note the windsock hanging limply in the background. This photograph was taken at Martuba, in Libya, on 21 February 1942 (*via Jerry Scutts*)

Iain Wyllie

Strapped into the snug-fitting confines of 'Yellow 14's' cockpit, Leutnant Marseille awaits the signal to start the engine on his 'Friedrich' at Martuba (*via Jerry Scutts*)

Marseille's Bf 109F-4/Z Trop Wk-Nr 12593 is prepared for refuelling from a mobile bowser at Martuba in early 1942. The rudder of this particular aircraft was painted primer red, with 50 kill symbols meticulously applied in yellow. Parked in the background is a Bf 108 'hack', which was frequently used by I./JG 27 during 1941-42 (*via Jerry Scutts*)

The South African pilots succeeded in getting amongst the dive-bombers prior to the Messerschmitt escorts intercepting them, and although no fewer than ten Ju 87s were claimed to have been destroyed, No 5 Sqn paid a heavy price for this success once they were engaged by 3./JG 27. Between 1322 and 1333 hours, six Tomahawks fell to the guns of *Staffelkapitän* 'Jochen' Marseille –

despite the fact the nose-mounted 20 mm cannon in his Messerschmitt fighter had jammed after he had fired just ten rounds. These kills took the 22-year-old oberleutnant's score to 75, and secured for him the coveted decoration of the Oak Leaves to his Knight's Cross.

One of the leading aces in North Africa by mid-1942, Marseille and the Bf 109 had forged an unbeatable partnership that few pilots (either Allied or Axis) could compete with in-theatre. He briefly explained his combat philosophy to the designer of his trusted weapon of war, Dipl-Ing Willy Messerschmitt, during an official visit that he made to the Bayerische Flugzeugwerke factory at Augsburg whilst on extended leave in Germany in early July 1942;

'I've fully integrated all the motions of air combat with difficult manoeuvres. It begins as I close with the enemy. I've now come so far that I can keep control of the Bf 109 in any situation, even in the tightest turns and at the lowest possible speeds. In combat I make all my motions unconsciously. This lets me concentrate fully on the attack, and fly my plane as though I had wings.'

Dubbed the 'Star of Afrika' by the German propaganda 'machine', Han-Joachim Marseille remained undefeated in action, for the North African aces of aces finally fell victim to a mechanical failure with one of his beloved Bf 109s on the last day of September 1942.

Heavy exhaust staining down the side of 'Yellow 14' denotes that 'Jochen' Marseille (at the extreme right of the photo) has been involved in combat over Ain El Gazala yet again during the spring of 1942. Between 21 February and 17 June his score doubled from 50 to 101 kills – and he was absent on leave in Germany for a full month during this period!

PILOT BIOGRAPHY – HANS-JOACHIM MARSEILLE

The son of an army major, when this young Berliner arrived at his first operational posting on the Channel coast, his superior officers were far from impressed by his bohemian, big city, mannerisms. Nor did the combat record of this jazz-loving oberfahnrich (Senior Officer Candidate) inspire much confidence, for although 'Jochen' Marseille claimed the destruction of seven RAF fighters, he was himself shot down four times in the process.

After being transferred from I./LG 2 to II./JG 52, Marseille was then shunted to I./JG 27 just prior to the unit's departure for North Africa. And it was over the open wastes of the Western Desert that he was to find true greatness. Indeed, the Hurricane he despatched over Tobruk on 23 April 1941 was but the first of an amazing succession of 150 further desert victories, which would make him the highest-scoring Luftwaffe fighter pilot ever to operate solely against the Western Allies.

Now master of his machine, Marseille concentrated on perfecting his tactics until he was expending on average only 15 bullets per kill! This, combined with his uncanny vision, led to his achieving multiple successes on many of his sorties. His most remarkable feat occurred on 1 September 1942 when he claimed no fewer than 17 kills.

Marseille's lengthening list of victories was recognised by a string of awards, culminating in the Diamonds to the Oak Leaves with Swords of his Knight's Cross on 2 September 1942. But by the last day of that month he was dead. Abandoning his favoured Bf 109F, he was for the first time flying a Bf 109G when its engine caught fire. Marseille bailed out, but was knocked unconscious by the tailplane. He fell to earth with his parachute unopened.

Hauptmann Hans-Joachim Marseille, *Staffelkapitän* of 3./JG 27 and the 'Star of Afrika', was no more. He was not yet 23 years old.

SPECIFICATION

Messerschmitt Bf 109F
(all dimensions and performance data for Bf 109F-4)

TYPE:	single-engined monoplane fighter
ACCOMMODATION:	pilot
DIMENSIONS:	length 29 ft 2.5 in (8.90 m) wingspan 32 ft 6.5 in (9.92 m) height 8 ft 6.5 in (2.60 m)
WEIGHTS:	empty 5259 lb (2390 kg) maximum take-off 6872 lb (3117 kg)
PERFORMANCE:	maximum speed 388 mph (624 kmh) range 528 miles (850 km) with external tank powerplant Daimler-Benz DB 601E-1 output 1350 hp (1007 kW)
ARMAMENT:	one 20 mm cannon in propeller hub and two 7.9 mm machine guns in upper cowling; F-4B fighter-bomber variant had provision for carriage of one 551-lb (250-kg) bomb under fuselage
FIRST FLIGHT DATE:	July 1940
OPERATORS:	Croatia, Germany, Hungary, Spain
PRODUCTION:	approximately 2200

Developed in response to the availability of the uprated Daimler-Benz DB 201N/E engine, the Bf 109F also exhibited much aerodynamic reworking in comparison with the Bf 109E. The engine cowl was appreciably smoother, the propeller hub enlarged, wing tips rounded off, rudder reduced in size, tailplane struts deleted and the tailwheel made to retract. The ailerons and flaps were also improved and the armament restricted to a single cannon and two machine guns, all of which were nose/engine mounted. The resulting fighter was undoubtedly the best handling Bf 109 of them all – it was also the most aesthetically pleasing of the many variants produced. The first production F-1s entered service on the Channel front in late 1940, and almost immediately revised versions with better armament and more powerful engines were put into production. Although a joy to fly, the F-model was criticised for its lack of firepower (particularly when compared with the Bf 109E-3/-4s that they were in the process of replacing), so some units carried out field modifications that saw two 20 mm cannon added in gondolas beneath the wings. The Bf 109F equipped two-thirds of the *Jagdwaffe* when Germany launched its assault on the USSR in June 1941, and the fighter also saw much action in North Africa in 1941-42. However, the introduction of the definitive Bf 109G in the early summer of 1942 resulted in the production of the F-model being immediately halted.

Bf 109F-4/Z Trop (Wk-Nr 10137) 'Yellow 14' of Oberleutnant Hans-Joachim Marseille, *Staffelkapitän* of 3./JG 27, Ain El Gazala, Libya, mid-June 1942

The future 'Star of Afrika' enjoyed a less than auspicious start to his career in-theatre, being forced to crash-land his shot up Bf 109E soon after downing his first kill over the desert. Marseille is believed to have written off at least seven Bf 109s during his brief time in the frontline, almost all of which wore his favourite ' Yellow 14' marking on their respective fuselages.

ACTION IN 'THE SLOT'

'He went down at a 45° angle. Bombers all go down the same way when you get them. There's a big burst of fire, which dies down, goes "whoooosh!" again, dies down, and repeats.'

Capt Joe Foss at the end of his Guadalcanal tour in early 1943. America's leading fighter ace at the time this photograph was taken, his image appeared on the cover of various magazines in the US, including *Life* and *True*. In the latter magazine, Foss received the following write-up; 'At Henderson, Foss always flew one of the chubby F4Fs, occasionally with the bravado number 13. His only lucky bit of clothing was an old hunting cap faded almost white. He liked to grow dark and scraggy goatees. He set his teeth on a cigar when he flew' (*via Peter Mersky*)

'I looked off in the distance and saw the bombers we were expecting. They were what we called Type I – twin-motored jobs resembling our B-25s somewhat. I climbed to meet them on a 180° course and made a run on the right rear bomber – the one on the right echelon. As I came down in a vertical dive, making my run and ready to shoot, he suddenly blew up. One of his tanks had exploded, though I hadn't fired a single shot. I later found out it was Ensign "Red" Thrash, a Navy pilot, who got him.

'I pulled through the pieces, moved up and shot at the next bomber. By that time I was too close for anything but a short burst, which started smoke but produced no fire or explosion.

'Then I dove and came up under the left wing of the V-formation, taking a belly shot at the last plane in line. It was a direct hit which caused an explosion and fire on the left motor. I was right under him, my nose pointing straight up, and the plane almost in a complete stall. It was impossible to miss. It was like pointing a pistol straight up in a room – you cannot help hitting the ceiling.

'He went down at a 45° angle. Bombers all go down the same way when you get them. There's a big burst of fire, which dies down, goes "whoooosh!" again, dies down, and repeats. Pretty soon a wing drops off and the bomber goes into a final spin.

'This one struck the water between Henderson Field and Tulagi, right in the middle of the channel. It went right on in full tilt, but three Japs out of the crew of six or seven lived. They didn't even have a scratch on them – nobody could figure it out.

'I returned to the field, ammunition gone, with Zeros in hot pursuit. I landed out of gas.'

This was how Medal of Honor winner Capt Joe Foss described the action on 18 October 1942 which gave him his fifth kill, and

Iain Wyllie

A VMF-121 F4F-4 prepares to land at Camp Kearney (which later became the site of Miramar Naval Air Station) in mid-1942. Under the command of Capt Leonard K Davis, the squadron operated in the San Diego area from March to August 1942. However, retaining full strength proved almost impossible owing to the near-constant transfers of pilots and aircraft to new units. Indeed, the squadron barely reached operating strength before embarking on the aircraft carrier USS *Copahee* with other elements of Marine Air Group 14 and heading for the South-west Pacific (*via the National Museum of Naval Aviation*)

Bearing the black side number 29, this VMF-121 F4F-4 taxies over Guadalcanal's pierced-steel matting in November 1942. By the time this photograph was taken, the squadron had been at 'Cactus' (the pilots' nickname for Henderson Field) for almost a month. The South Pacific climate quickly bleached out aircraft colours, whilst Guadalcanal's alternately muddy and dusty environment, coupled with austere maintenance facilities, left aircraft with a decidedly 'hang-dog' appearance (*via the National Museum of Naval Aviation*)

ace status. The extract is taken from the wartime volume, *Joe Foss, Flying Marine*, which was co-written with Walter Simmons and published in 1943.

Flying from Henderson Field with VMF-121, Foss had quickly become adept at staying alive in the deadly skies over Guadalcanal. Indeed, he had become so proficient in the art of aerial combat that he had scored the prerequisite five kills to secure 'acedom' within nine days of his arrival in-theatre!

Joe Foss flew two sorties on 18 October in defence of US naval vessels traversing the treacherous stretch of water known to American servicemen as 'The Slot'. He initially tangled with a large formation of Zeros that were providing top cover escort for G4M 'Betty' torpedo-bombers from the Misawa Naval Air Group.

In the ensuing dogfight a single Wildcat was lost, although Foss swiftly exacted revenge by downing a pair of Imperial Japanese Navy fighters in quick succession, and leaving a third trailing smoke. He then latched onto the torpedo-bombers and shot a further two aircraft down.

By the time Joe Foss had finished his tour of duty with VMF-121 in late January 1943, his tally had risen to 26 kills, thus making him the first US pilot to equal the score of ranking American World War 1 ace, Eddie Rickenbacker.

'Joe's Flying Circus' pose in front of a suitably-decorated F4F-4 bearing the strictly non-regulation nickname *MARINE SPECIAL* on its engine cowling. This shot was almost certainly taken at the auxiliary field east of Henderson known variously as the 'fighter strip' or 'cow pasture'. Joe Foss is seen standing second from left (*via Peter Mersky*)

PILOT BIOGRAPHY – JOE FOSS

A South Dakota farm boy who had become a skilled hunter and crack shot by his mid-teens, Joe Foss entered the Marine aviation programme in 1940. Upon being designated a naval aviator in March of the following year, his efforts to join a fighter squadron were continually stymied by his above average ability as a pilot – Foss's superiors felt he was of greater use to the 'Corps serving as an instructor. Finally, after constant requests, he was posted to Wildcat-equipped VMF-121 in mid-1942. Promoted to captain soon after his arrival, Foss had become the unit's Executive Officer by the time it was thrust into combat from Henderson Field, on Guadalcanal, on 9 October.

Joe Foss's hunting instincts soon came to the fore, and in just 63 days of combat, he succeeded in destroying 26 aircraft (19 of which were A6M Zero-sen fighters). Shot down just once in this time, he contracted malaria in mid-November and was evacuated with the surviving members of VMF-121 on the 19th of that month. Only partially recuperated, he returned to Guadalacanal in January, and succeeded in destroying three more Zero fighters before finally returning to the USA. Awarded the Congressional Medal of Honor by President Franklin D Roosevelt in May 1943, Foss was prevented from seeing further action due to recurring bouts of malaria.

Postwar, he rose to the rank of brigadier-general in the South Dakota Air National Guard, served two terms as the Governor of his home state in the 1950s and became a well-known television sports commentator. Latterly, Joe Foss has also been president of numerous organisations ranging from the National Society of Crippled Children and Adults to the National Rifle Association.

F4F-4 BuNo 03450/white 50 of Capt Joseph Jacob Foss, VMF-121, Guadalcanal, November 1942

This aircraft was used by the Marine's ranking ace to down at least one of the 19 Zeros he destroyed during his Guadalcanal tour. Foss had a great respect for the Mitsubishi naval fighter, being quoted as saying, 'If you're alone and you meet a Zero, run like hell – you're outnumbered'. BuNo 03450 was entirely representative of 'Cactus Air Force' Wildcats in 1942-43, bearing no personal or unit markings. Foss's logbook reveals that he flew no fewer than 34 different Wildcats during his tour in the Solomon Islands, and claimed kills in ten of them.

SPECIFICATION

Grumman F4F Wildcat
(all dimensions and performance data for F4F-4)

TYPE:	single-engined monoplane fighter
ACCOMMODATION:	pilot
DIMENSIONS:	length 28 ft 9 in (8.76 m)
	wingspan 38 ft 0 in (11.58 m)
	height 11 ft 4 in (3.45 m)
WEIGHTS:	empty 5895 lb (2674 kg)
	maximum take-off 7952 lb (3607 kg)
PERFORMANCE:	maximum speed 320 mph (515 kmh)
	range 770 miles (1239 km)
	powerplant Pratt & Whitney R-1830-76/86
	Twin Wasp
	output 1200 hp (895 kW)
ARMAMENT:	six 0.50 in machine guns in wings; provision for
	two 250-lb (113-kg) bombs under wings
FIRST FLIGHT DATE:	2 September 1937
OPERATORS:	UK, USA
PRODUCTION:	7808

Derived from a biplane design offered in competition to the more modern Brewster F2A Buffalo monoplane, the Wildcat was the result of a study undertaken by Grumman into the feasibility of a single wing naval fighter. Designated the XF4F-2, it lost out to the rival Brewster in the fly-off due to the latter's superior handling qualities. However, Grumman reworked the prototype into the vastly superior XF4F-3 of March 1939, fitting a more powerful Twin Wasp engine with a two-stage supercharger, increasing the fighter's wing span and redesigning its tail surfaces. After flight trials, the Navy ordered 78 F4F-3s, which they christened the Wildcat. Entering service at the end of 1940, the Wildcat proved to be a worthy opponent for the Japanese A6M Zero-sen during the great carrier battles of 1942-43 and the invasion of Guadalcanal. The aircraft was also a popular addition to the Royal Navy's Fleet Air Arm, who used various marks from 1940 through to VE-Day. By 1943 General Motors (GM) had commenced building F4F-4s, which they redesignated FM-1s. Later that same year GM switched production to the FM-2, which utilised a turbocharged Wright R-1820-56 Cyclone in place of the Twin Wasp. This swap made for a higher top speed and an optimum altitude some 50 per cent greater than that achieved in the FM-1 – by the time production was terminated in August 1945, no fewer than 4467 FM-2s had been built.

DUKE OF 92

'The dive-bomber went down in spirals and exploded upon hitting the ground. Its demise was observed by most of the squadron.'

'The squadron patrolled over Tripoli–Benito in the afternoon at about 10,000 ft, 12 Spitfires taking part in the operation. This was our first show over this area, and bloody accurate flak from Castel Benito caused some panic. Soon afterwards I spotted some Ju 87s bombing our troops while we were patrolling in the Tripoli area. I immediately reported them to our wing leader, Wg Cdr John Darwen. The squadron had not spotted them, so I dived after eight of the Ju 87s, which were flying in two vics of three and one of two.

'I felt rather exposed approaching the formation of Stukas on my own, and for a time, until the squadron arrived, I had them all to myself, returning my fire and doing stall turns around me at a height of about 1000 ft near Castel Benito aerodrome. I closed astern of the starboard vic and attacked the aircraft at the extreme right. He broke away sharply before I had closed on him and had a chance to fire. I altered my attack and went after the No 3 Ju 87 in the third vic. I opened fire at between 100 and 200 yards, and although I observed DeWilde strikes, these seemed to do little damage to the dive-bomber. The Ju 87 formation then completely

Flt Lt Neville Duke poses with his suitably-marked Spitfire VB 'QJ-R' (either ER821 or ES121) at Bu Grara in mid-March 1943. The kill markings painted beneath the windscreen of this fighter had been added by the ace's groundcrew (*via Norman Franks*)

With its 'QJ' codes barely visible to the right of the roundel, Mk VB EP442 was photographed by Neville Duke during its time with No 92 Sqn in early 1943. This aircraft was lost on 19 March 1943 when it crashed east of Sorman West airfield, on the Tripoli coast, during an operational flight in bad weather (*via Norman Franks*)

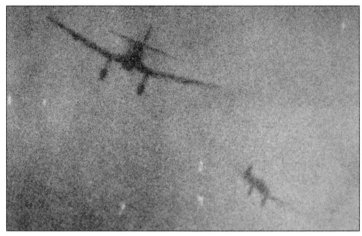

This gun camera footage was taken by Flg Off Duke during the engagement in which he shot down a Ju 87D from III./StG 3 on 21 January 1943 – the very action depicted in Iain Wyllie's artwork (*via Norman Franks*)

At the front. This photograph, again taken by a young Flg Off Duke, shows pilots from No 92 Sqn at rest between sorties in the patch of coastal desert that served as the unit's rudimentary dispersal area at El Nogra, in Libya, in December 1942. The Mk VB in the background (ER338) was used by Neville Duke to claim his 11th and 12th kills – Italian Macchi C.202 fighters – on 11 January 1943. A veteran of service with Nos 92, 601 and 225 Sqns, as well as the Blida Training Flight in Algeria, ER338 survived the war only to be scrapped in August 1946 (*via Norman Franks*)

broke up, each aircraft making steep climbs and stall turns and dives.

'I attacked a second Ju 87 from astern at 100 yards slightly to starboard, and observed cannon shells burst in the starboard wing root, which burst into flames. The dive-bomber went down in spirals and exploded upon hitting the ground. Its demise was observed by most of the squadron.

'"Nice show", said Darwen when we got back to Wadi Surri. "I didn't see those chaps for a start. That makes your twelfth doesn't it?"

'I said it did (postwar research has revealed that this was actually Duke's thirteenth kill – Ed).

'"Good show. Well your promotion to flight lieutenant has come through. You'd better come over to my trailer to wet your new stripe this evening".

'I was now "A" Flight commander in No 92 Sqn and enjoying life. I subsequently got legless with my CO, the boss of No 3 Sqn RAAF and WingCo Darwen in his trailer that night.'

Flying Spitfire VB ER220, Flg Off Neville Duke had engaged Ju 87Ds of III./StG 3 during this action, which had taken place on 21 January 1943. The aircraft that the Spitfire ace had attacked crashed in the Tarhuna area, and although he had initially believed his opponents to be Italian Stukas, an examination of the wreckage of 'his' Ju 87 revealed that the dive-bombers were indeed German. The pilot of Duke's Stuka actually succeeded in bailing out of his stricken aircraft, but was killed when his parachute failed to open. A further two Ju 87Ds were downed during this one-sided fight by fellow No 92 Sqn aces Flt Lt 'Sammy' Samouelle and Flg Off Milt Jowsey.

PILOT BIOGRAPHY – NEVILLE DUKE

Born in Tonbridge, Kent, Neville Duke joined the RAF in 1940, and in April of the following year was posted to No 92 Sqn at Biggin Hill. By the end of August he had claimed two enemy aircraft destroyed and a further two damaged (all Bf 109Fs), and he was quickly picked out as a talented novice.

In November 1941 Duke was posted to No 112 Sqn in North Africa, and flying firstly the Tomahawk and then the Kittyhawk, he rapidly built up his score. Having completed his first tour by February 1942, he served as an instructor at the fighter School at El Ballah, in Egypt, before returning to No 92 Sqn as a flight commander in November of that same year. Operating Spitfire VB Trops, the unit saw much action during the invasion of Tunisia, and Duke continued to claim victories. Following the end of his second tour in June 1943, he was then promoted to squadron leader, and spent a further period at a training unit at Abu Sueir, again in Egypt, as its Chief Flying Instructor.

In March 1944 he assumed command of No 145 Sqn, flying Spitfire VIIIs, in Italy, and by September Duke had become the top scoring RAF fighter pilot in the Mediterranean theatre.

He returned to the United Kingdom in October 1944 and was allocated to Hawker Aircraft Ltd as a production test pilot. After the war Duke attended a course at the Empire Test Pilots School, then joined the RAF High Speed Flight in June 1946. In 1948 he left the service and returned to Hawker to work as a test pilot where, in 1951, he became Chief Test Pilot. Whilst in that post he carried out much of the early test flying of the company's successful Hunter jet fighter, the highlight of which was setting a new world speed record in 1953. Still an avid private pilot (and sailor) to this day, Neville Duke lives with his wife Gwen in retirement in Lymington, Hampshire.

Spitfire Mk VB Trop ER220/'QJ-R' of Flg Off Neville Duke, No 92 Sqn, Waddi Surri, Libya, late January 1943

Delivered to No 9 Maintenance Unit (MU) at RAF Cosford on the last day of August 1942, this aircraft was subsequently passed on to No 47 MU at Sealand two weeks later. Here, it was prepared for shipping to North Africa, and then loaded aboard the vessel *Empire Liberty* along with a number of other Mk VB Trops. The aircraft departed British shores on 19 September, and according to its record card, was next noted at No 116 MU's aircraft assembly facility at Takoradi, on the Gold Coast, on 7 November. ER220 was issued to No 92 Sqn as an attrition replacement in November 1942, and its arrival coincided with Neville Duke's posting to the unit after a six-month spell 'resting' at the Middle East Fighter School. He would go on to score two kills in the aircraft, his first claim being against a C.202 that he downed near Zidan, in Tunisia, on 8 January. He followed this with the Ju 87 victory described in this chapter. ER220 was passed on to No 601 Sqn soon afterwards, and was shot down by a Bf 110 from III./ZG 26 off Cap Bon, on the Tunisian coast, on 17 April 1943. Its pilot, Flt Sgt P F Griffiths, bailed out over the sea and was subsequently captured.

SPECIFICATION

Supermarine Spitfire Mk V
(all dimensions and performance data for Spitfire Mk VB/C)

TYPE:	single-engined monoplane fighter
ACCOMMODATION:	pilot
DIMENSIONS:	length 29 ft 11 in (9.12 m)
	wingspan 36 ft 10 in (11.23 m)
	height 11 ft 5 in (3.48 m)
WEIGHTS:	empty 5100 lb (2313 kg)
	loaded weight 6785 lb (3078 kg)
PERFORMANCE:	maximum speed 374 mph (602 kmh)
	range 470 miles (756 km)
	powerplant Rolls-Royce Merlin 45/50/55/56
	output 1470 hp (1096 kW)
ARMAMENT:	four 0.303 in machine guns and two 20 mm cannon in wings (VC had provision for two or four 20 mm cannon in wings); provision for one 500-lb (227-kg) or two 250-lb (113-kg) bombs externally
FIRST FLIGHT DATE:	December 1940
OPERATORS:	Australia, Canada, Egypt, France, Greece, Italy, New Zealand, Portugal, South Africa, Turkey, UK, USA, USSR
PRODUCTION:	6472 Mk Vs

As the first Spitfire variant to see extensive service outside of Britain, the Mk V fought the Axis alliance not only on the Western Front, but over North Africa, the Mediterranean, Australasia and the Eastern Front. The first attempts by Supermarine to upgrade the Mk I/II had resulted in the production of two Mk IIIs, the latter fighter boasting a 1390 hp Merlin XX, revised airframe, stronger undercarriage, clipped wings and a retractable tailwheel. However, all these improvements combined to slow down the production rate of the desperately needed fighter, so an order for 1000 was cancelled, and the much simpler Mk V was chosen instead. Getting the improved aircraft into the frontline was a matter of great importance, as the arrival of new German fighters (the Bf 109F and the Fw 190A) on the Channel front had rendered the early marks ineffective. In order to speed up the delivery process, the Mk V had been created by simply pairing a Mk I or II fuselage with the new Merlin 45 engine – the combination proved to be so successful that some 6479 airframes would eventually be built. Thanks to this overwhelming production run, the Mk V bore the brunt of fighter operations on virtually all fronts to which the RAF was committed between 1941 and late 1943.

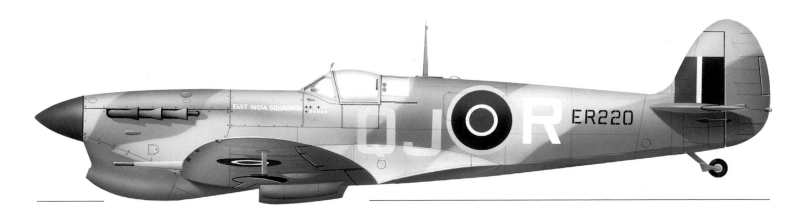

My Hardest Dogfight

'A few tiny specks emerge from the mist in the far distance. They quickly get bigger and reveal themselves as a gaggle of 20 Soviet ground-attack aircraft.'

'This area, dotted with several Soviet landing strips, has always been a good hunting ground in the past. We don't have to wait long today either. Ahead to the left, a few tiny specks emerge from the mist in the far distance. They quickly get bigger and reveal themselves as a gaggle of 20 Soviet ground-attack aircraft. A few moments later we spot six more machines, American fighters, flying escort.

'We are flying at about 1000 m, the Soviets are some 200 m below us – their escort at about 1200 m. I immediately climb to get above them. The sun is in the south-west. The "Americans", now below me, haven't noticed anything. I get one in my sights and open fire – he immediately dives away on fire, hitting the ground in a burst of flame. Startled, the remaining five curve away to the right. I have achieved my object. The fighters are now some 500 to 600 metres away from the ground-attackers, and my men have a clear field.

'Meanwhile, as I try for another fighter, they are attempting to get on my tail. They end up in a circle, with me in the middle trying to get into position for a good shot. We are all gradually

This portrait of the Luftwaffe's fifth-ranking ace, Walter Nowotny, was taken soon after he had been awarded the Knight's Cross (proudly worn around his neck) on 4 September 1942. His score stood at 56 victories at this point, and by the time he was killed in action on 8 November 1944, Nowotny's tally had risen to 258 (*via John Weal*)

losing height. I hardly fire a shot, while behind me one or two of the opposition loose off wildly at me – at much too great a range and far wide of the mark. Then, at about 50 m off the ground, I get the second one in my sights. He too immediately goes into the ground in a ball of flame.

'I look over my shoulder. The fight has taken a nasty turn. Eight Soviet fighters have arrived on the scene and join in the proceedings! I am sitting on the tail of one of the "Americans". Behind me is one of the Soviets. A few quick glances convince me he is getting closer. To my right a line of bullet holes suddenly appears in my wing. The Soviet is letting fly with everything he has got. His firing hardly stops. A cannon shell smashes into my wing, tearing open the surface. Ivan is getting closer and closer. He's almost within ramming distance. Whenever I glance behind me, the huge Soviet star seems to fill my vision. Bullets continue to hit my wing. They are getting closer to my cockpit.

'The moment of decision has come. I take one last chance and dump as much speed as I dare. I use all the skill and expertise I have gained in my many previous dogfights to hold her steady as my speeds sinks suddenly and dangerously low.

'Fifty metres ahead of me is the "American". Little more than ten metres behind me the Russian. Throughout the chase I have been slipping to the right in an attempt to dodge my pursuer's shots. I try the same manoeuvre one last time. And this time Ivan falls for it. For a split-second, as I wallow once more to the right at little more than a stall, he loses concentration. I take two more cannon hits before I complete the manoeuvre, but then he has overshot me, flashing past beneath my wings.

'He appears ahead of me. I clearly see the pilot in his cockpit, the Soviet star. I ram home the throttle – full power! I hope the good old Focke–Wulf, hurt though she is, can take it! Within a trice I am on top of the Russian. He goes down under my first burst of fire. The duel is over. The whole fight has lasted exactly 45 minutes.'

A factory-fresh I./JG 54 Fw 190A-4 has its engine run up by its pilot prior to the fighter flying the first sortie of the day from Krasnogvardeisk in early 1943. The gentle mottling of the winter white camouflage is clealy visible from this angle, as is the fact that the groundcrew have painted out the yellow theatre band that once surrounded the fuselage cross. Note also the carbon deposits from the starboard MG 151 20 mm cannon, which denote that this aircraft has very recently seen action (via John Weal)

With the dials in his cockpit indicating a problem with his engine following a brief run up, the pilot has shut down the Fw 190A-4's BMW and called over his 'black man' for a consultation on what to do next. Had his radial powerplant 'warmed to the occasion', the pilot would have waved away both the trolley acc, parked alongside the fighter, and the wheel chocks, before taxying away from the snow-covered dispersal area (via John Weal)

PILOT BIOGRAPHY – WALTER NOWOTNY

One of the many Austrians to rise high in the ranks of the wartime Luftwaffe, Walter Nowotny flew almost exclusively against the Russians. He was arguably the most successful Fw 190 pilot on the Eastern Front, with all but three of his 258 confirmed kills being achieved against the Soviets.

He joined III.*Gruppe* of JG 54 in February 1941, and his first three victories – a trio of I-153 biplanes claimed over the Baltic Sea on 19 July of that year – were very nearly his last. Forced to ditch, the 20-year-old Nowotny barely survived the following 72 hours in an open dinghy before being washed ashore. By the autumn of 1942 his scored had topped the 50 mark, he had been awarded the Knight's Cross, and he was serving as the *Staffelkapitän* of 1./JG 54. But it was in the summer of 1943 that his combat career really took off.

In June 1943 Nowotny claimed 41 kills, including ten in one day. In August he was made *Gruppenkommandeur* of I./JG 54, and he celebrated his promotion by scoring 49 victories during this month alone! In September his tally reached 200, and on 14 October 1943 he became the first Luftwaffe fighter pilot to achieve 250 kills. Nowotny was honoured with the Diamonds to the Oak Leaves with Swords of his Knight's Cross.

In the autumn of 1944, following a spell commanding a fighter training school, Major Nowotny was selected to head an experimental Me 262 jet fighter unit – *Kommando Nowotny*. On 6 November, following unmistakable sounds of aerial combat from above, pilots from Nowotny's unit, watching from their Achmer base, saw their leader's machine emerge from solid cloud and dive vertically into the ground. He had been killed attempting to engage US heavy bombers.

SPECIFICATION

**Focke-Wulf Fw 190A
(all dimensions and performance data for Fw 190A-3)**

TYPE:	single-engined monoplane fighter
ACCOMMODATION:	pilot
DIMENSIONS:	length 29 ft 0 in (8.84 m) wingspan 34 ft 5.5 in (10.50 m) height 13 ft 0 in (3.96 m)
WEIGHTS:	empty 6393 lb (2900 kg) maximum take-off 8770 lb (3978 kg)
PERFORMANCE:	maximum speed 382 mph (615 kmh) range 497 miles (800 km) output 1700 hp (1268 kW)
ARMAMENT:	two 7.9 mm machine guns in nose, four 20 mm cannon in wings
FIRST FLIGHT DATE:	1 June 1939
OPERATORS:	Germany, Turkey
PRODUCTION:	19,379 (all models)

Arguably Germany's best piston-engined fighter of the war, the Fw 190 caught the RAF by surprise when it appeared over the Channel Front in 1941. Indeed, the Focke-Wulf fighter remained unmatched in aerial combat in the west until the advent of the Spitfire Mk IX in late 1942 and the La-5FN and Yak-9 on the Eastern Front in early 1943. Powered by the compact BMW 801 radial engine, the Fw 190 also boasted excellent handling characteristics to match its turn of speed. A-model Fw 190s were the dedicated fighter variants of the 'butcher bird', and as the design matured, so more guns were fitted and more power squeezed out of the BMW engine. By the end of 1942, production of the Fw 190 accounted for half of all German fighters built that year, and the fighter-bomber F/G had also been developed – the first F-models entered frontline service on the Eastern Front during the winter of 1942-43. All manner of ordnance from bombs to rockets could be carried by the fighter-bomber Fw 190, and additional protective armour for the pilot was also added around the cockpit. Variants of the Fw 190 saw action against the Allies on all fronts of the war in Europe, and the aircraft remained a deadly opponent for Allied fighter pilots right up to VE-Day.

Walter Nowotny flew this Fw 190A-4 whilst serving as *Staffelkapitän* of 1./JG 54 in the winter of 1942-43. It is seen approaching the icy strip at Krasnogvardeisk with the legendary ace at the controls. The Russians had become quite proficient at staging surprise hit and run raids on the Luftwaffe's airfields by early 1943, and take-offs and landings became times of great peril for Fw 190 pilots. Amongst the first things taught to new arrivals in the east was how to take-off from any position on the field, either from a standing start or taxying, and how to land quickly and safely from a low-level formation. Here, Nowotny does the latter, skimming in over a large snow bank at the runway threshold (*via John Weal*)

Fw 190A-4 'White 8' of Leutnant Walter Nowotny, *Staffelkapitän* 1./JG 54, Krasnogvardeisk, November 1942

A well-documented machine, in stark contrast to the majority of the anonymous and unidentifiable Fw 190s flown on the Eastern Front by all and sundry (or at least by whoever's name happened to be next on the ops board), this is the aircraft in which Nowotny scored his *Staffel's* 300th victory of the war. The toned-down – or simply dirty – white of the fuselage cross seems an unnecessary precaution on an otherwise standard white winter camouflaged A-4.

JABO HUNTERS

'Turning steeply to port and looking down, I saw the enemy aircraft going down in a 30° dive, almost on his back. He was then at about 300 ft, and was emitting clouds of thick black smoke.'

Plt Off 'Pinkie' Stark smiles for the camera soon after completing the sortie that saw him down No 609 Sqn's 200th victory of the war. Aside from feeling satisfied at having added another kill to his – and the squadron's – tally, he was also rather pleased to have won the not inconsiderable sweepstakes which had been awaiting the lucky pilot to down the 200th aircraft. Stark's victim on this day (5 October 1943) was a Ju 88 caught at low-level during a 'Ranger' south of Soissons (*L W F Stark via Chris Thomas*)

'At 0945 hours I took off as Yellow 2 with Sgt Leslie as Yellow 1, and we proceeded on north to the South Foreland patrol.

'At about 1015 hours we received information from Hornchurch that 2 plus bandits were proceeding in an easterly direction, ten miles north-east of Calais. At this time we were about six miles east of Dover, going south. We turned east at increased speed in search of the bandits. A few minutes later we were informed that they had turned south-west, and later by "Swingate", that they were heading east again. We thereupon decided to abandon the chase and turned north-west. Immediately afterwards, Sgt Leslie saw four aircraft approaching from behind on our port side. We both turned sharply to port and temporarily lost sight of the other aircraft in the sun. We finally got within range just off the French coast between Dunkirk and Mardyck, and I recognised two of the enemy aircraft as Fw 190s. These two were flying in line astern at between 500 and 600 ft, going west, parallel to the coast about 200 yards offshore.

'I attacked the leading machine, opening fire at about 100 yards

from astern. I saw strikes on the fuselage and starboard wing. Several objects fell off the aircraft, and flames appeared round the cockpit. Quite a large area appeared to be flaming. He turned slowly to port, and I pulled up to avoid collision. Turning steeply to port and looking down, I saw the enemy aircraft going down in a 30° dive, almost on his back. He was then at about 300 ft, and was emitting clouds of thick black smoke. In my own opinion the enemy aircraft was well on fire, although the flames were then obscured by the altitude of the aircraft and the clouds of smoke. I am certain that he could not possibly have recovered from the inverted dive at that low altitude, but I did not observe any further results as my attention was then taken up by the second machine, which was coming round on my tail. I continued my turn to port,

Iain Wyllie

This is the aircraft that Flt Sgt 'Pinkie' Stark was flying on the occasion of his first victory, which is depicted in Iain Wyllie's painting within this chapter. Coded 'PR-F', and wearing the name *Mavis* just forward of the cockpit, this aircraft was not Stark's usual aircraft at this time – between January and June 1943, 'PR-J'/R8715 features most often in his logbook. Stark's victim on 12 March was Feldwebel Emil Boesch, flying Fw 190 'Black 12' (Wk-Nr 0829) of 10(*Jabo*)./JG 54 (*IWM*)

Pilots of No 609 Sqn pose outside their Manston dispersal hut in the spring of 1943. Flt Sgt 'Pinkie' Stark is standing in the middle row of three pilots at the extreme right. His CO, and legendary ace, Sqn Ldr R P 'Bee' Beamont, is stood in the centre of the doorway (*L W F Stark via Chris Thomas*)

and fired two bursts at a third Fw 190, which twice crossed in front of me – once from the starboard side and then from the port side. I did not observe any hits on this aircraft.

'The second machine was still behind us, so I continued turning tightly to the left. He fired several bursts at me, but could not get quite enough deflection. Then I felt strikes on my own aircraft, and oil began to flow freely around the cockpit. About this time he climbed up, still turning with the apparent intention of getting a height advantage, and as he came down again, I tightened my turn still more, and saw Sgt Leslie make an attack on him. He then climbed away into the sun, and finally disappeared, Sgt Leslie and myself returning to base. The whole of this engagement took place just over the beach between Dunkirk and Mardyck.

'On landing, I found two bullet holes in my machine – one in the oil tank, which entered about 18 inches below the windscreen on the port side of the cockpit, and one through the rudder trimming-tab.

'I wish to claim the enemy aircraft, previously claimed "probable", as "destroyed".'

A head-on view of DN406, taken at RAF Manston in the spring of 1943. Prior to serving with No 609 Sqn, this aircraft had spent time with Nos 198 and 257 Sqns, and after seeing considerable action with the auxiliary unit, it was passed on to No 56 Sqn. Well and truly worn out by the late summer of 1943, DN406 was struck off charge on 31 August 1943 and scrapped (*IWM*)

PILOT BIOGRAPHY – LAWRENCE 'PINKIE' STARK

Born in Bolton, Lancashire, 'Pinkie' Stark joined the RAF in 1940 midway through an apprenticeship with Metropolitan-Vickers in Manchester. Trained in Canada, he served as a Staff Pilot at No 10 Air Gunnery School upon his return to the UK in mid-1941. Helping air gunners achieve proficiency with turret gun-firing, Stark flew Defiants in this rather unglamorous role for a full year, before being posted to No 56 Operational Training Unit. He joined No 609 Sqn in early 1943, and subsequently became one of the few aces to score all his kills flying Typhoons.

Awarded a DFC in March 1944, Stark had by then been posted to No 263 Sqn, where he served as a flight commander until shot down by flak over Brittany on 3 July. He evaded capture, and upon his return to the UK was sent to Gloster Aircraft Company to serve as a production test pilot on Typhoons. A Bar to his DFC was announced during September of 1944. Having been sufficiently rested, Stark was sent back to the frontline in March 1945, serving initially as a flight commander with No 164 Sqn, and then assuming command of No 609 Sqn.

Following the auxiliary unit's disbandment in September 1945, he performed staff duties in Germany before joining the Aeroplane & Armament Experimental Establishment. Stark was employed as a test pilot at Boscombe Down for over three years, before resuming frontline flying as a flight commander with No 32 Sqn in the Middle East. More test flying followed this squadron tour, and he eventually retired from the RAF in November 1963. In civilian life, 'Pinkie' Stark managed Rochester Airport for 25 years, and today he lives in retirement in nearby Bredhurst, near Gillingham.

SPECIFICATION

**Hawker Typhoon
(all dimensions and performance data for Typhoon Mk IB)**

TYPE:	single-engined monoplane fighter
ACCOMMODATION:	pilot
DIMENSIONS:	lenght 31 ft 11 in (9.73 m) wingspan 41 ft 7 in (12.67 m) height 15 ft 3.5 in (4.66 m)
WEIGHTS:	empty 9800 lb (4445 kg) maximum take-off 13,980 lb (6341 kg)
PERFORMANCE:	maximum speed 412 mph (659.2 kmh) range 980 miles (1577 km) with external tanks powerplant Napier Sabre IIA output 2180 hp (1626 kW)
ARMAMENT:	four 20 mm cannon in wings; provision for two 500-lb (227-kg) or 1000-lb (454-kg) bombs or eight 3-in/60-lb (7.62-cm/27-kg) rockets under wings
FIRST FLIGHT DATE:	24 February 1940
OPERATORS:	Canada, New Zealand, UK
PRODUCTION:	3317

The Typhoon was the RAF's first production fighter capable of achieving speeds in excess of 400 mph in level flight. However, the brutish Hawker design was almost deemed a failure right at the start of its career when the combination of poor climb and altitude performance, unreliability of its new Napier Sabre engine (chosen in favour of the cancelled Rolls-Royce Vultee/Hawker Tornado combination) and suspect rear fuselage assembly cast serious doubts over its suitability for frontline service. Refusing to give up on the aircraft, Hawker and Napier spent over a year (from mid-1941 through to mid-1942) 'beefing up' the airframe and correcting engine maladies to the point where the Typhoon was found to be an excellent low altitude fighter – it effectively neutralised the Luftwaffe's Fw 190 'hit and run' raiders, which had frequently terrorised the south coast of England in 1942-43. The Typhoon's proven ability at low-level also made it the ideal platform for the ground attack mission, its quartet of 20 mm cannon and deadly array of rockets and bombs allowing pilots to roam the skies over occupied western Europe attacking all manner of targets from ships to tanks. One of the key weapons in the Allied arsenal for Operation *Overlord*, the Typhoon equipped more than 20 units by mid 1944. The last example of Hawker's original Napier-engined fighter was built in November 1945.

Typhoon Mk IB SW411/'PR-J' of Sqn Ldr L W F Stark, OC No 609 Sqn, Plantlunne (B.103), Germany, May 1945

Having completed a tour with No 609 Sqn in 1943-44, 'Pinkie' Stark returned to the unit in March 1945 as its last wartime commanding officer. For much of his time with the squadron, he retained SW411 as his personal aircraft, flying his first mission in it on 19 March 1945 and his last in September when No 609 Sqn disbanded. The gloss black and yellow spinner worn by this aircraft was applied soon after VE-Day. The inner surfaces of the undercarriage doors were also finished in yellow, with white edging. Stored at No 5 MU at Kemble for a year, SW411 was finally scrapped in October 1946.

SW411 PR • J

First Corsair Ace

'The times that I really got into trouble came about due to the Zero that I didn't see, and conversely, I'm sure that with most of the kills I got they didn't see me.'

'Being the first unit to go into action in the Corsair, we didn't know exactly how to employ it, so we had to establish a doctrine. We knew that there would be many other Corsair squadrons following us, and they would want to know what we did, and how we did it. They would then be able to augment our experience and develop their own tactics. I had asked one very experienced Wildcat pilot, who had made a great name for himself during the early days of Guadalcanal, how to go about combat with the Zero. All he said was "you've gotta' go after them". Well, we knew it would take more than that!

'I learned quickly that altitude was paramount. Whoever had altitude dictated the terms of the battle, and there was nothing a Zero pilot could do to change that – we had him. The F4U could out-perform the Zero in every aspect except slow speed manoeuvrability and slow speed rate of climb. Therefore, you avoided getting slow when combating a Zero. It took time, but

1st Lt Kenneth Ambrose Walsh prepares for a combat mission. Selected for Naval Flight Training in March 1936, he had experienced seven years of frontline flying by the time he deployed to Guadalcanal with VMF-124 in February 1943. He became the first Corsair ace (flying BuNo 02310) three months later, on 13 May 1943, when he downed two Zeros 15 miles east of Russell Island – this is the action depicted in Iain Wyllie's painting (*via Peter Mersky*)

This official photograph of Ken Walsh was taken in the New Hebrides on 4 September 1943 – just five days after the Corsair ace had claimed his 20th, and last, kill with VMF-124. Dubbed the 'Fighting Irishman of Marine Aviation' by the press, he was shipped home to America soon after posing for this shot, having completed his third frontline tour in seven months (*via Peter Mersky*)

Ken Walsh is seen running up one of his 'No 13s' (his favoured side number) on 1 September 1943 at the former Japanese airfield at Munda (*via Jim Sullivan*)

eventually we developed tactics and employed them very effectively.

'When we were accustomed to the area, and knew our capabilities, there were instances when the Zero was little more than a victim. I came to know the Zero, and I learned how to attack it. Being in my seventh consecutive year of frontline flying, I knew how to fire the guns and how to use our Mk 8 gunsight. The guns were boresighted to 1000 ft. The electric sight had rings covering so many mils, 1000 ft equalling one mil. We had six 0.50-cal guns with 400 rounds per gun, and a rate of fire of 800 rounds per minute. Our belt loading was one incendiary, one tracer and one armour piercing. A two-second burst would fire 150 rounds, and the Zero, like most Japanese aircraft, had no armour plating or self-sealing tanks. So, if you hit them, they'd burn, with their aluminium construction including magnesium parts, which added further fuel to the fire. You can imagine what would happen if you got 30 or 40 hits on them.

'There were times, however, that I tangled with a Zero at slow speed, one-on-one. In these instances I considered myself fortunate to survive a battle. Of my 21 victories, 17 were against Zeros, and I lost five aircraft as a result of combat. I was shot down three times, and I crashed one that ploughed into the line back at base and wiped out another F4U. I was shot-up at least a dozen times, but usually the aeroplane could be repaired. The times that I really got into trouble came about due to the Zero that I didn't see, and conversely, I'm sure that with most of the kills I got they didn't see me. So, when new units came up behind us we told them what we had learned. Everything was a calculated risk, but I had a lot more to tell them about than just "you gotta' go after them!"'

PILOT BIOGRAPHY – KEN WALSH

A native of Brooklyn, New York, Ken Walsh enlisted in the US Marine Corps in 1933. Serving initially as an aircraft mechanic and radioman, he was accepted for flight training in 1935 and posted to a series of scout and observation squadrons following his designation as a Naval Aviation Pilot. Walsh saw sea time aboard USS *Yorktown*, *Wasp* and *Ranger* up until he transferred to fighters (F4F-3 Wildcats) in mid-1941 following the formation of VMF-121. He joined VMF-124 in September of the following year, and was commissioned as a second lieutenant soon after.

The unit debuted the new F4U Corsair in combat when it was sent into action at Guadalcanal in February 1943, and by 13 May Ken Walsh had become the type's first ace. He completed three combat tours with VMF-124, claiming 20 kills, 2 probables and 1 damaged, and was himself shot down once. He returned to the USA in September 1943, and in February of the following year Walsh received the Congressional Medal of Honor from President Franklin D Roosevelt. Following a spell as an instructor, now Capt Walsh returned to action with VMF-222 in April 1945, flying fighter-bomber missions over Samar and Okinawa – he added a single aerial victory to his tally in June.

Postwar, he remained in the 'Corps, seeing further action over Korea with VMR-152 in 1950-51, before finally retiring with the rank of lieutenant-colonel in 1962. Aside from his Medal of Honor, Ken Walsh's awards included the Distinguished Flying Cross with six Gold Stars, the Air Medal with fourteen Gold Stars and the Good Conduct medal with one Bronze Star. Kenneth Ambrose Walsh passed away on 30 July 1998, aged 81.

SPECIFICATION

Vought F4U Corsair
(all dimensions and performance data for F4U-1D)

TYPE:	single-engined monoplane fighter
ACCOMMODATION:	pilot
DIMENSIONS:	length 32 ft 9.5 in (9.99 m)
	wingspan 40 ft 11.75 in (12.49 m)
	height 15 ft 0.25 in (4.58 m)
WEIGHTS:	empty 8873 lb (4025 kg)
	maximum take-off 13,846 lb (6280 kg)
PERFORMANCE:	maximum speed 392 mph (631 kmh)
	range 1562 miles (2514 km)
	powerplant Pratt & Whitney R-2800-8
	Double Wasp
	output 2000 hp (1491 kW)
ARMAMENT:	six 0.50in machine guns in wings; two 1000-lb (454-kg) bombs or eight rocket projectiles externally
FIRST FLIGHT DATE:	29 May 1940
OPERATORS:	New Zealand, UK, USA
PRODUCTION:	12,571 (all models)

Designed as a lightweight fighter built around the most powerful piston engine then available, Vought's prototype XF4U-1 was ordered by the US Navy in June 1938 following a study of their V-166 proposal. In order to harness the immense power of the Pratt & Whitney XR-2800 Double Wasp engine, the largest diameter propeller ever fitted to a fighter up to that point in aeronautical history had to be bolted to the front of the prototype – sufficient ground clearance for the prop was achieved through the use of a distinctive inverted gull wing. The future look rosy for the aircraft, but modifications incorporated into the design as a result of lessons learned in combat over Europe detrimentally affected the Corsair. As a result of these problems, it was left to land-based Marine Corps units to debut the aircraft in combat in February 1943 – the Royal Navy's Fleet Air Arm also commenced operations with the Corsair that same year, but crucially from the decks of carriers. By mid-1944 Vought had rectified the handling problems, and the Corsair was declared suitable for deck operations with the US Navy. Unlike other navy fighters, the F4U enjoyed a prosperous postwar career, with both Vought- and Goodyear-built aircraft remaining in service until after the Korean War. Indeed, the final F4U-7 (built for the French *Aéronavale*) did not roll off the Vought production line until 31 January 1952, this aircraft being the 12,571st Corsair built.

F4U-1 Corsair *My Bonnie* of VMF-124 throws up a spray of water from Munda's runway in August 1943 following a tropical storm. Possibly an ex-VMF-213 aircraft, this Vought fighter has two false gun ports painted on each wing. This practice was carried out by VMF-124's armourers in an attempt to convince the Japanese that the Corsair was more heavily armed than it actually was! (*via Peter Mersky*)

F4U-1 white 13 of 1Lt Kenneth A Walsh, VMF-124, Munda, New Georgia Island, September 1943

Ken Walsh flew this aircraft towards the end of his third tour. Its two-tone paint scheme consisted of Blue Grey upper surfaces with Light Grey undersurfaces, except for the folding portion of the wing, where the upper surface colour was also used. The fighter has a white 13 painted aft of the canopy and field-applied bars added to the national insignia on the wing surfaces. Following this tour, Ken Walsh became a Training Command instructor at NAS Jacksonville, Florida, before returning to combat in April 1945 with VMF-222.

FIRST OF MANY

'The Zero fighter, because of its low wing loading, has superior manoeuvrability to all our present service type aircraft. Never attempt to dogfight the Zero.'

This portrait of PO Hiroyoshi Nishizawa was taken at Lae, New Guinea, in 1942 (*via Henry Sakaida*)

On 7 June 1943, Japan's third-ranking ace, Chief Petty Officer (CPO) Hiroyoshi Nishizawa of the 251st Air Group (AG), encountered the F4U Corsair for the first time in combat. This aircraft was a quantum improvement over the previous Allied fighters that he had engaged during the Japanese advance through the South Pacific. Faster, more manoeuvrable and better armed than the Wildcats, Warhawks and Airacobras he had claimed in great numbers since May 1942, the Marine Corsair proved a worthy opponent. Indeed, he had been told that the mighty F4U was unbeatable when its pilot employed 'hit and run' tactics. Nishizawa was not to be intimidated, however, and he was eager to take on the gull-winged fighter.

Part of a force of 81 A6M3 Model 22 Zeros sortied by the 251st AG from the fortress at Rabaul in support of a major Japanese counter-offensive launched on this day, Nishizawa intercepted both US Marine Corps and Royal New Zealand Air Force (RNZAF) fighters. In the aerial melée which ensued, four Corsairs from VMF-112 and a solitary RNZAF P-40 were lost, with the Japanese ace claiming a single example of each type destroyed.

From June through to 21 August 1943, CPO Nishizawa would engage F4Us on a regular basis over Rendova, Buin and Vella Lavella, as the Allies slowly pushed northwards towards Rabaul. During this period, he participated in the destruction of 45 Corsairs, which were attributed to his unit rather than to him, as per the Japanese Naval Air Force GHQ directive prohibiting individual victory credits.

With an eventual tally of 86 kills, Hiroyoshi Nishizawa graphically proved just how effective the Mitsubishi A6M Type 0 was in skilled hands. As the JNAF's staple fighter throughout World War 2, it was flown by the vast majority of the 183 pilots who scored five or more kills between mid-1940 and August 1945. The Type 0 was easily the best aircraft of its type in-theatre on either side at the time of the Pearl Harbor attack on 7 December 1941, and it remained in the ascendancy until the P-38 Lightning and F4U Corsair began to appear in significant numbers in the South-west Pacific from early 1943 onwards.

Iain Wyllie

Early encounters with the Type 0 in the first year of the war saw Allied units suffer serious losses at the hands of the more experienced Japanese fighter pilots. Indeed, things got so bad that the US Informational Intelligence Service issued the following notice to all army air force, navy and marine corps fighter units in the Pacific in December 1942;

'The Zero fighter, because of its low wing loading, has superior manoeuvrability to all our present service type aircraft. It is necessary to maintain a speed of over 300 mph (260 knots) indicated to successfully combat this airplane. Never attempt to dogfight the Zero. Never manoeuvre with the Zero at speeds below 300 mph indicated unless directly behind it. Never follow a Zero into a climb at slow speeds. Service types will stall out at the steep angle where the Zero has reached its most manoeuvrable speed. At this point it is possible for the Zero to complete a loop, putting it in a position for a rear-quarter attack.'

ABOVE Mechanics labour over an A6M2 Model 21 at Lakunai airfield as Mt Hanabuki belches smoke in the background – the active volcano was a familiar landmark for pilots approaching Rabaul. Field modifications performed on the Zero included sawing off the radio mast and removing the useless radio in order to save weight. This volcano and vulcan crater erupted in September 1994, burying downtown Rabaul and Lakunai Airfield under tons of ash (*Maru via Henry Sakaida*)

BELOW LEFT Tainan AG 2nd Squadron pilots are seen at Rabaul in 1942. In the front row, from left to right, are PO3/c Yoshizo Ohashi, PO3/c Seiji Ishikawa (5 victories) and PO3/c Kenichi Kumagai (2 victories). In the second row, left to right, are PO2/c Toshio Ota (34 victories), PO1/c Saburo Sakai (60+ victories) and Seaman 1/c Masayoshi Yonekawa (6 victories). Standing, from left to right, are PO1/c Hiroyoshi Nishizawa (86 victories), PO3/c Daizo Fukumori, PO3/c Yutaka Kimura and PO3/c Masuaki Endo (14 victories). Of the pilots featured in this group photograph, only Sakai survived the war (*via Henry Sakaida*)

BELOW A6M3a Zero 22s of the 251st AG are seen in a rare air-to-air photograph heading out on a patrol from Rabaul in 1943. The tail code of this fighter was originally UI-105, but at various times the prefix 'UI' was painted out with the hastily-applied green daubed over the remainder of the aircraft's previously grey fuselage. This particular fighter was one of many flown by veteran ace Hiroyoshi Nishizawa, and it seen here carrying a 330 l (72.6 Imp gal) drop tank (*Maru via Henry Sakaida*)

PILOT BIOGRAPHY – HIROYOSHI NISHIZAWA

Born on 27 January 1920 in Nagano Prefecture, Hiroyoshi Nishizawa joined the navy in June 1936 and completed flying training in March 1939.

When the Pacific War began, Nishizawa was flying Japanese Naval Air Force (JNAF) Type 96 'Claudes' with the Chitose AG in the Marshall Islands, and he duly accompanied the group to Rabaul, where he joined the 4th AG in February 1942. When elements of the Tainan AG arrived at Rabaul from the Dutch East Indies in April, Nishizawa was transferred into the 2nd Squadron, where he found himself in the company of PO1/c Saburo Sakai. The latter tutored the gaunt and sickly loner, together with PO2/c Toshio Ota, and together the threesome became famous as the 'Cleanup Trio'.

In November, surviving pilots of the Tainan AG were transferred to the 251st, with those few who had survived the combats over Guadalcanal being held in high esteem by the JNAF. In September the 251st AG was re-rolled as a nightfighter unit, and PO1/c Nishizawa was transferred to the 253rd AG, based at Tobera Airfield (Rabaul). The following month he was ordered back to Japan to serve as an instructor as part of the JNAF's efforts to cure their fighter pilot shortage.

He hated his new assignment, likening it to baby-sitting, and after repeated requests for a combat assignment, he was transferred to the 201st AG in the Philippines in time to participate in the counter-attack against the American naval fleets.

On 26 October 1944 he boarded a Ki-49 bomber and left Cebu Island for Mabalacat (near Clark Field) to pick up some replacement Zeros. A frantic SOS radio message was received from the transport, but it failed to arrive at its destination. The aircraft had been shot down by two Hellcats from VF-14 that were in the process of returning to their aircraft carrier, the USS *Wasp*. Lt(jg) Harold P Newell was one of those pilots credited with the destruction of the bomber, and in 1982 he recounted the action;

'I stayed below a thin stratus cloud layer and my wingman stayed on top. The aircraft popped out of the clouds slightly to my right in a left hand turn. It was at close range and I opened fire. After several short bursts the port engine and inboard wing section were in flames. The aircraft went into an increasingly steep diving left turn and I continued firing until the fuselage started shedding pieces and the fire increased.'

There were no survivors.

A6M3a Model 22 of CPO Hiroyoshi Nishizawa, 251st AG, Aichi Prefecture, Japan, early Spring 1943

The unit designation 'UI' was used from 1942 through to June 1943, during which time Hiroyoshi Nishizawa flew this aircraft as an instructor. The standard JNAF light grey scheme worn by this fighter was hastily camouflaged with foliage green paint within days of the 251st arriving in Rabaul.

SPECIFICATION

Mitsubishi A6M2/3 Zero
(all dimensions and performance data for A6M2 Model 21)

TYPE:	single-engined monoplane fighter
ACCOMMODATION:	pilot
DIMENSIONS:	length 29 ft 8.75 in (9.06 m)
	wingspan 39 ft 4.25 in (12.00 m)
	height 10 ft 0.15 in (3.05 m)
WEIGHTS:	empty 3704 lb (1680 kg)
	maximum take off 6164 lb (2796 kg)
PERFORMANCE:	maximum speed 331 mph (533 kmh)
	range 1930 miles (3105 km) with external tanks
	powerplant Nakajima NK1C Sakae 12
	output 950 hp (708 kW)
ARMAMENT:	two 7.7 mm machine guns in nose,
	two 20 mm cannon in wings; provision
	for two underwing 132-lb (60-kg) bombs
FIRST FLIGHT DATE:	1 April 1939
OPERATORS:	Japan
PRODUCTION:	4335

Undoubtedly the most famous Japanese combat aircraft of World War 2, the A6M was developed by Mitsubishi to meet a demanding JNAF requirement for a replacement to the successful A5M of the late 1930s. Officially designated the Navy Type 0 Carrier Fighter *Rei-sen* ('Zero Fighter'), the A6M offered an impressive mix of high performance, long range and superb manoeuvrability, all in a lightweight and modestly powered airframe. The first two prototype A6M1s were powered by the relatively underpowered and undeveloped Mitsubishi Zuisei 13 engine, and a switch was soon made to the Sakae, which it retained until war's end. Redesignated the A6M2, the first production-standard Model 11s were delivered to the JNAF in July 1940, and barely two months later the variant saw action over China when 13 Zeros tangled with 27 Polikarpov I-15s and I-16s and shot them all down without suffering a single loss! Production switched to the Model 21 at around the same time, this variant having folding wingtips for deck elevator compatibility. A6M2s made up no less than two-thirds of the JNAF's fighter force by 7 December 1941, and 135 Zeros took part in the Pearl Harbor assault. By then the re-engined A6M3 was just entering production, the new variant being powered by a supercharged Sakae 21 rated at 1130 hp (843 kW). This variant also dispensed with the folding wingtips, leaving the wings with a 'squared off' appearance. A6M3 production finally ended in mid-1943.

'RED 1'

'The Gustavs *in my Flight are becoming sluggish to handle under the heavy load of stovepipes, as well as everything else that has to be carried.'*

In the painting opposite, Major Hermann Graf is seen diving away in his Bf 109G-6 Wk-Nr 15913 'Red 1' just seconds after performing a head-on attack on a formation of B-17Fs from the 92nd Bomb Group (BG) on 6 September 1943. His pass has left one Flying Fortress streaming smoke from its outer port engine. The 92nd lost seven bombers during this mission, at least one of which almost certainly fell to Major Graf – he claimed two B-17s.

The Eighth Air Force targeted Stuttgart on this day, despatching over 400 'heavies' for the very first time. However, the mission proved both costly and ineffective for the Americans, with 45 bombers being lost and the target left untouched due to increasing cloud. The 'heavies' ended up attacking 'targets of opportunity' instead, dropping ordnance over wide tracts of Germany and occupied western Europe – the 100th BG, for example, dropped its bombs south-west of Paris!

As previously detailed, Hermann Graf was amongst those *Jagdflieger* to benefit from the fragmentation of the American bomber formations. A veteran of the air war over the Eastern Front, where he had claimed 172 kills in just 13 months, Graf had been recalled from training command in August 1943 to head the specialist Defence of the Reich unit JG(r) 50, based at Wiesbaden-Erbenheim. It was tasked with combating US heavy bombers, as well as high-flying RAF reconnaissance aircraft, and for this dual role the *Geschwader* equipped its Bf 109G-6s either with

Major Hermann Graf, Eastern Front ace and the first pilot in the world to achieve the double 'century', also commanded JGs 50, 1 and 11 in Defence of the Reich, where he was credited with ten victories (*via John Weal*)

underwing rockets (as depicted in this artwork) or additional cannon gondolas.

Graf brought down at least two B-17s while leading JG(r) 50, and when that unit was disbanded in November he was appointed *Kommodore* of JG 11. The first rocket-armed Bf 109G-6s had made their frontline debut in August 1943 with the fifth *staffel* of this *geschwader*, which at the time was commanded by innovative bomber destroyer Oberleutnant Heinz Knoke. He made the following observations about the weapon, and the effect it had both on his Messerschmitt and the American 'heavies' he was targeting, in his classic autobiography, *I Flew for the Führer*;

'15 August 1943 – Our aircraft are rigged under each wing with objects whose strange appearance causes them to be given the name of "stovepipes". These are, in fact, ejection tubes for a kind of eight-inch mortar shell, or rather a rocket, consisting of a propellant charge, an explosive charge and a time fuse. At this rate we shall soon find ourselves carrying heavy artillery. The idea seems to be for our Flights to form up at a range of 2500 ft behind the enemy formations, and then use the contraptions for firing explosive rockets at them.

'19 August 1943 – The *Gustavs* in my Flight are becoming sluggish to handle under the heavy load of stovepipes, as well as everything else that has to be carried.

'27 September 1943 – Enemy concentrations in map reference sector Dora-Dora. I order all our rockets discharged when we are in formation at a range of 2000 ft. The next moment a simply fantastic scene unfolds before my eyes. My own two rockets both

A main weapon in the Bf 109G's anti-bomber armoury was the 210 mm air-to-air rocket. These unidentified early Reich's defence G-6s, with rockets already loaded in their underwing launch tubes, await the 'heavies'' approach (*via John Weal*)

From this angle it is clearly obvious why the rocket tubes bolted onto the G-6 were dubbed 'stovepipes' by *Gustav* pilots. Although giving the Bf 109 a far greater 'punch' when attempting to knock down heavily-armed American four-engined bombers, the rockets were not overly liked by German pilots, as they drastically reduced the manoeuvrability of the Messerschmitt fighter (*via John Weal*)

register a perfect bull's-eye on a Fortress. Thereupon, I am confronted with an enormous solid ball of fire. The bomber has blown up in mid-air with its entire load of bombs. The blazing, smoking fragments come fluttering down.'

JG(r) 50's Leutnant Gottfried Weiroster enjoys all the comforts of home at Wiesbaden-Erbenheim courtesy of the 'U.S. AIR CORPS'! (*via Jerry Scutts*)

PILOT BIOGRAPHY – HERMANN GRAF

For the fighter pilot who was the first in the world to score 200 kills, who received Germany's highest decoration when a 29-year-old oberleutnant, and who ended the war as *Kommodore* of JG 52 (the most successful fighter unit ever in terms of aerial victories), the name of Hermann Graf is now surprisingly little known to all but a few.

Although he joined JG 51 in the early months of the war, a subsequent stint as a fighter instructor meant that Leutnant Graf did not achieve his first victory until August 1941 when serving with JG 52 on the Eastern Front. But within little over a year after that, he was wearing the Diamonds – awarded on 16 September 1942 for 172 aircraft destroyed. Graf was one of only seven day fighter pilots so honoured.

By now a national hero, the one-time apprentice blacksmith was able to indulge his life-long passion for football. Graf formed his own team, 'The Red Hunters', and whenever he was posted to a new unit he ensured that his star players accompanied him!

In 1943 Graf served another spell in training command, before heading the specialist unit JG(r) 50 and JG 11 in Defence of the Reich duties. This netted him ten heavy bombers before he returned to JG 52 in the east in October 1944, this time as *Kommodore*. By war's end he had amassed a total of 212 aerial victories.

It was during the immediate postwar years of Soviet captivity that the pragmatic Graf's actions contributed to his own downfall. Unlike others, such as the redoubtable Erich Hartmann, Graf co-operated – some say collaborated – with his captors. After his release in 1950 and return to Germany, he was ostracised by many of his former comrades. Although most have since mellowed, Hermann Graf has been fated to remain something of a 'non-person' in Luftwaffe history. He died in his home town of Engen, in Baden, in November 1988, aged 76.

SPECIFICATION

Messerschmitt Bf 109G
(all dimensions and performance data for Bf 109G-6)

TYPE:	single-engined monoplane fighter
ACCOMMODATION:	pilot
DIMENSIONS:	length 29 ft 7.5 in (9.03 m)
	wingspan 32 ft 6.5 in (9.92 m)
	height 8 ft 2.5 in (2.50 m)
WEIGHTS:	empty 5893 lb (2673 kg)
	maximum take off 7496 lb (3400 kg)
PERFORMANCE:	maximum speed 386 mph (621 kmh)
	range 620 miles (998 km) with external tank
	powerplant Daimler-Benz DB 605AM
	output 1800 hp (1342 kW)
ARMAMENT:	one 20 mm cannon in propeller hub, two 13 mm machine guns in upper cowling and two 20 mm cannon under wings; provision for various underfuselage and underwing stores
FIRST FLIGHT DATE:	late summer 1941
OPERATORS:	Bulgaria, Croatia, Finland, Germany, Hungary, Italy, Romania, Slovakia, Switzerland
PRODUCTION:	23,500 G-models

The Bf 109G combined the F-model's refined airframe with the larger, heavier and considerably more powerful 1475 hp DB 605 engine to produce the most successful Messerschmitt fighter variant of them all. Cockpit pressurisation was also introduced for the first time with the G-1, although most later sub-variants lacked this feature. Produced in staggering numbers from early 1942 until war's end, some 23,500 Bf 109Gs were constructed in total – including an overwhelming 14,212 in 1944. Numerous modifications to the basic G-1 were introduced either in the factory (as *Umrüst-Bausätze* factory conversion sets) or in the field (*Rüstsätze*), and these included provision for extra armament, additional radios, introduction of a wooden tailplane, the fitting of a lengthened tailwheel and the installation of the MW50 water/methanol-boosted DB 605D engine. In an attempt to standardise the equipment of the frontline force, Messerschmitt produced the Bf 109G-6 in late 1942, and this model included many of these previously ad hoc additions. Unfortunately, the continual adding of weighty items like wing cannon and a larger engine to the once slight airframe of the Bf 109 eliminated much of the fighter's manoeuvrability, and instead served to emphasise the aircraft's poor low speed performance, lateral control and ground handling.

Bf 109G-6 (Wk-Nr 15913) 'Red 1' of Major Hermann Graf, *Gruppenkommandeur* JG(r) 50, Wiesbaden-Erbenheim, September 1943
This G-6 *'Kanonenboot'* was the mount of Major Hermann Graf during his tenure of office as *Kommandeur* of the single *Gruppe*-strong JG(r) 50 in the late summer/early autumn of 1943. The rudder meticulously records all of Graf's Eastern Front victories, the number 172 (for which he received the Diamonds), surmounted and surrounded by his initials

and the award ribbon, plus two rows of 15 individual bars each. The last three bars are for recent western successes, including the two B-17s downed on 6 September. Hermann Graf would claim a total of ten four engined bombers in Defence of the Reich operations before returning to the east, and his old unit, JG 52.

SEVEN DOWN

'I was closing so fast that the only way to bring my guns to bear was to roll the P-38 tightly left, to an almost inverted attitude.'

Maj Bill Leverette had been in command of the 14th Fighter Group's 37th Fighter Squadron for little more than a month when just after noon on 9 October 1943, he commenced an engagement which would result in him achieving a record score for a US Army Air Force pilot in a single mission. In his first encounter with the enemy, the major claimed seven aircraft destroyed and two damaged!

Leverette was leading two flights of P-38Gs on a patrol over the Aegean Sea when he spotted a large formation of Ju 87D Stukas attacking Royal Navy vessels bombarding the German and Italian garrisons on the island of Rhodes. He recounted what happened next to American aviation historian Eric Hammel;

'Before the Germans knew we were there, I attacked the nearest enemy aeroplane ahead of me. I fired a short burst with the .50s from about 20°. Smoke poured from the left side of the Stuka's engine.

'The Stuka pilots who still had bombs aboard jettisoned them once the shooting started. As soon as I saw the smoke coming from the first Stuka, I broke to my left and attacked a second Stuka from its rear and slightly below. After I fired a short burst from about 200 yards, this aeroplane rolled over and spiralled steeply downward.

'I broke away to the left again and turned back toward the formation of Stukas. As I did, I saw both Stukas that I had already fired on strike the water. I attacked a third Stuka from a slight angle off its left rear. I opened fire at this aeroplane just as the rear

This photograph of leading Army Air Force 'ace-in-a-day', Bill Leverette, was taken during his time as a flying cadet in early 1940 (*via John Stanaway*)

Iain Wyllie

gunner fired at me. The gunner immediately ceased firing, and I saw the pilot jump out of the aeroplane, although I did not see his parachute open. The gunner did not get out.

'I continued on into the enemy formation and attacked another Stuka – my fourth – from an angle of 30°. I observed cannon and machine-gun fire hit the Stuka's engine, and I saw large pieces of cowling and other parts fly off. The engine immediately began smoking profusely, and the Stuka nosed down.

'I broke away upward and to my left, and then I re-entered the enemy formation. Another Stuka was nearly dead ahead. I opened fire again with my cannon and machine guns from an angle of about 15°. The canopy and various parts of this Stuka flew off, and a large flame shot out of the engine and from along the left wing root. The gunner jumped out of the aeroplane as I passed it.

'Continuing into the formation, I approached a sixth Stuka from below and to his left rear, but on a crossing course that would take me over to the right rear, heading slightly away from it. I was closing so fast that the only way to bring my guns to bear was to roll the P-38 tightly left, to an almost inverted attitude. As my guns lined up on the Stuka momentarily, I opened fire at very close range and observed concentrated strikes on the upper right side of the engine. The engine immediately began to smoke, and I broke away slightly to my left.

'I attacked the seventh Stuka from straight behind and slightly below. The rear gunner fired at me briefly, but he stopped as soon as I fired a short burst of my own. As the Stuka nosed slightly down, I closed to minimum range and fired a short burst into the bottom of the engine and fuselage.'

ABOVE Lt Harry Hanna (right) was a part of Maj Leverette's flight during the Stuka massacre of 9 October 1943, and he was credited with downing five of the dive-bombers in the melée. These were his only successes during his 50-mission tour, and earned him the DFC. His CO was awarded the Distinguished Service Cross, which is second only to the Congressional Medal of Honor (*via John Stanaway*)

LEFT Now a fully-fledged fighter ace, Maj Leverette (left) poses with fellow 37th FS pilot Bob Margison at Gambut-2 airfield, in Libya, in late 1943. The latter individual was credited with one of the Ju 87s downed during the epic 9 October 1943 mission, and also observed many of the splashes left by Leverette's seven victims after they had hit the sea (*via John Stanaway*)

PILOT BIOGRAPHY – BILL LEVERETTE

A native of Palatka, Florida, Bill Leverette joined the army reserve in September 1934, having obtained a degree in mechanical engineering prior to signing up. He served in the infantry until 1939, when he transferred to the army air corps. Rated a pilot in March 1940, Leverette flew P-39s with the 31st Pursuit Group and 53rd and 338th Fighter Groups in the USA, before transferring to the 14th FG in North Africa in August 1943.

By this stage a very experienced pilot, but having yet to test his mettle in combat, Leverette joined the 37th FS, flying P-38 Lightnings. And despite having seen no action, he was made CO of the unit just weeks after his arrival in the Mediterranean Theater of Operations (MTO). He had little real affection for the big Lockheed fighter, which he claimed was tiring to fly, but nevertheless enjoyed great success during his tour. Aside from the seven Ju 87Ds that he destroyed on 9 October, Leverette also claimed two Bf 110s and two Bf 109s before leaving the 14th FG in April 1944.

He remained in the postwar air force, rising to the rank of full colonel. Bill Leverette commanded the France-based 48th Fighter-Bomber Wing, equipped with F-86F Sabres, in 1955, and finally retired from the USAF in December 1965.

A P-38F has its engines run up at Liverpool's Speke Airport in January 1943, soon after arriving in the UK by ship from the USA. Once deemed fit for frontline flying, the aircraft was duly sent out to North Africa for service in the MTO with the Twelfth Air Force (*via John Stanaway*)

P-38H (serial unknown) *Stingeree* **of Maj William L Leverette, CO of the 37th FS/14th FG, Gambut-2, Libya, October 1943**

Named after a southern American variation of the stingray, this P-38H was used by William Leverette (a native of Florida, hence the 'fishy' nickname) to claim most, if not all, of his 11 aerial victories. The seven Ju 87s that he was credited with on 9 October 1943 constituted a record for American pilots in Europe. This astounding tally has often been questioned by ex-pilots and historians alike, but Leverette assured Osprey author John Stanaway that one of the P-38 pilots in his formation descended to low altitude over the becalmed sea in order to confirm numerous splashes in the water made by the crashing Stukas. Once the latter individual had returned to base, the number of splashes he reported was consistent with the tally of kills claimed by the successful P-38 pilots.

SPECIFICATION

Lockheed P-38H Lightning

TYPE:	twin-engined monoplane fighter
ACCOMMODATION:	pilot
DIMENSIONS:	length 37 ft 10 in (11.53 m) wingspan 52 ft 0 in (15.85 m) height 9 ft 10 in (3.00 m)
WEIGHTS:	empty 12,380 lb (5615 kg) maximum take-off 20,300 lb (9208 kg)
PERFORMANCE:	maximum speed 402 mph (643.2 kmh) range 2400 miles (3840 km) with external tanks powerplants two Allison V-1710-89/-91 engines output 2850 hp (2126 kW)
ARMAMENT:	one 20 mm cannon and four 0.50 in machine guns in nose; maximum bomb load of 4000 lb (1814 kg) under wings
FIRST FLIGHT DATE:	27 January 1939 (XP-38)
OPERATORS:	USA
PRODUCTION:	601 (including 128 F-5C photo-recce variants)

The P-38 Lightning was Lockheed's first venture into the world of high performance military aircraft. Keen to break into the lucrative military marketplace, the company had eagerly responded to the USAAC's 1937 Request for Proposals pertaining to the acquisition of a long-range interceptor. Aside from its novel twin-boom and central nacelle layout, the prototype XP-38, as it was designated by Lockheed, utilised butt-joined and flush-riveted all-metal skins (and flying surfaces) – a first for a US fighter. The XP-38's test programme progressed well, and aside from some minor adjustments to the flying surfaces and introduction of progressively more powerful Allison engines, frontline P-38s differed little from the prototype throughout the aircraft's six-year production run. The appellation 'Lightning' was bestowed upon the P-38 by the RAF when the type was ordered in 1940, and duly adopted by the Americans the following year. The near-identical G- and H-model P-38s proved to be the real workhorse variants of the Lightning in the MTO, being issued to Twelfth and Fifteenth Air Force fighter groups from the autumn of 1943 onwards. Used primarily as bomber escorts, the Lockheed fighters roamed all over the Mediterranean thanks to the aircraft's impressive range. And no fewer than 37 aces scored five or more kills in the MTO with the Lightning, making it the most successful fighter in-theatre in 1943-44.

'CHECKERTAIL CLAN'

'I saw the Ju 88 and gave him a damned good chase. I finally caught up with him, gave him a burst and saw him crash and burn.'

Lt Col Bob Baseler and his personal P-47D-23 *BIG STUD* (42-75008) are seen at Lesina, in Italy, in early 1944 (*via Dennis Kucera*)

On the morning of 30 January 1944, the 325th Fighter Group (FG) sortied every available P-47 Thunderbolt from its sprawling Foggia base, in southern Italy, and headed north. Crossing the Adriatic Sea at low level so as to keep well below radar detection height, the famous 'Checkertail Clan' was heading for a surprise sweep of Axis airfields in the Villaorba and Udine areas of northern Italy. Following in their wake would be 215 B-17s and B-24s from the Fifteenth Air Force's heavy bomber groups.

Leading the Republic fighters on this long-range mission was the group's commanding officer, Lt Col Robert Lee 'Bob' Baseler. The flight north was plagued with haze over the sea, obscuring the horizon as the group sped towards the target. One of the mission participants was nine-kill ace Capt Frank J Collins;

'We flew so low, prop wash sprayed up behind each plane the way it does behind an outboard motor boat. Altimeters were set at zero, and we never got above 50 ft.'

Baseler's skill as an aviator was born out when the 325th cleared the mist and sighted the Italian coast once again. Despite navigating entirely by dead reckoning, he discovered that the formation was in exactly the right spot at precisely the right time. As the P-47s crossed the enemy coastline, he initiated a long climb in order to allow the Thunderbolt pilots to commence dive-bombing runs on the target from between 15,000 and 19,000 ft.

And although the Luftwaffe's radar operators soon picked up the approaching 'heavies', they failed to detect the P-47s. This resulted in almost complete surprise being achieved over both airfields, 60 white-starred fighters screaming down in power dives. The attack was led by aircraft of the 319th FS, with the 317th to the left and the 318th on the right. Winging over from 19,000 ft, the Thunderbolt pilots watched a mass of enemy aircraft frantically scrambling to take off from the airfield. Opening the attack shortly before noon, the 325th enjoyed what amounted to a 35-minute 'turkey shoot'.

Flying his famous P-47D-10 *BIG STUD* on this occasion, Bob Baseler soon sighted a lone Ju 88 flying to the east of Palmanova. Although having already 'made ace' in the P-40F with the 325th FG during engagements with German and Italian forces over North Africa and Sardinia, the lieutenant-colonel had failed to score a kill in the P-47 since the big Republic fighter replaced the Warhawk in the autumn of 1943. This was about to change. Baseler was particularly pleased to spot 'his' Junkers bomber, for it was the only time he ever encountered a multi-engined enemy aircraft in flight.

BIG STUD was perhaps the most famous of all the 'Checkertail' Thunderbolts, Bob Baseler leading the 325th FG in this aircraft during the group's legendary airfield raid on 30 January 1944 (*via via Dennis Kucera*)

A seasoned pre-war fighter pilot who had flown P-35s, P-36s and P-39s by the time he was made CO of the 325th FG's 319th FS in August 1942, Bob Baseler is remembered by his colleagues as being a 'tall, red-headed, easy going type with a ready sense of humour' (*via Jerry Scutts*)

'I saw the Ju 88 and gave him a damned good chase. I finally caught up with him, gave him a burst and saw him crash and burn', Baseler later recounted.

As the 325th FG caused mayhem over the target at 'zero feet', 76 B-17s droned into view to release their loads from 23,000 ft. Deadly showers of fragmentation bombs – 10,988 of them – exploded over Villaorba.

The mission proved to be a great success for the 'Checkertail Clan', whose pilots were credited with downing 38 Axis aircraft for the loss of two P-47s. This was the group's largest single-mission claim for the war, and resulted in it receiving its second Distinguished Unit Citation. Lt Col Bob Baseler was also honoured with the Silver Star for his outstanding leadership during this raid, the award being pinned to his chest by Gen Nathan F Twining, Commander of the Fifteenth Air Force, just minutes after he had landed back at Foggia!

Baseler carried the name *STUD* on all of his aircraft in the MTO, the first of which was a P-40F. This was followed by this P-47D, which he of course called *BIG STUD*, then a P-51B christened *LITTLE STUD* and finally a B-17 named *SUPER STUD*! (*via Dennis Kucera*)

PILOT BIOGRAPHY – BOB BASELER

Hailing from Ardmore, Pennsylvania, Robert Lee 'Bob' Baseler joined the Army Air Corps' air reserve in early 1938. He undertook his flight training at Kelly Field, Texas, between 1 March 1938 and 1 February 1939, after which he was posted to the 1st Pursuit Group's 94th Pursuit Squadron. Baseler flew both Seversky P-35s and Curtiss P-36A Hawks during his time with the 1st PG at Selfridge Field, Michigan, before moving to the 24th PS/16th PG in the Panama Canal Zone in August 1939. Based at Albrook Field, on the Pacific side of the canal, Baseler once again found himself at the controls of the P-36.

Transferring into the regular army during his time in Panama, Baseler spent the last few months of his time with the 24th PS flying Bell P-39D Airacobras. He returned to the USA in August 1941, and spent a year instructing, before receiving orders to join the newly-formed 319th FS as its CO. Part of the recently-activated 325th FG, the unit was equipped with P-40F Warhawks and sent to North Africa aboard the aircraft carrier USS *Ranger* in December 1942.

The 325th FG flew directly from the ship to Casablanca, in French Morocco, and commenced combat operations in April 1943. By this time Bob Baseler was the group's Executive and Operations Officer, and he became one of its first aces on 26 July when he claimed his fifth kill. Promoted to command the 325th earlier that same month, he remained its CO until 1 April 1944, overseeing the group's transition to the P-47. Baseler then became Assistant Chief of Staff to Brig-Gen Dean C Strother, Commander of the 306th Fighter Wing, which controlled the 325th.

Serving in the air force postwar, Col Baseler finally retired in June 1962. He lost a long battle with cancer in July 1983, passing away at the age of 71.

SPECIFICATION

Republic P-47D Thunderbolt

TYPE:	single-engined monoplane fighter
ACCOMMODATION:	pilot
DIMENSIONS:	length 36 ft 1.75 in (11.02 m)
	wingspan 40 ft 9.5 in (12.43 m)
	height 14 ft 8 in (4.47 m)
WEIGHTS:	empty 9950 lb (4513.3 kg)
	maximum take-off 17,500 lb (7938.0 kg)
PERFORMANCE:	maximum speed 433 mph (696.8 kmh)
	range 1900 miles (3060 km) with external tanks
	powerplant Pratt & Whitney R-2800-59W
	Double Wasp
	output 2535 hp (1890.3 kW)
ARMAMENT:	eight 0.50 in machine guns in wings; two 1000-lb (454-kg) or three 500-lb (227-kg) bombs or ten 5 in (12.7 mm) rockets externally
FIRST FLIGHT DATE:	6 May 1941 (XP-47B)
OPERATORS:	Brazil, France, Mexico, UK, USA, USSR
PRODUCTION:	12,065

The original P-47 design was produced to meet a 1940 USAAC requirement for a lightweight interceptor similar in size and stature to the Spitfire and Bf 109. Powered by Allison's ubiquitous V-1710-39 1150 hp inline engine, the XP-47A was to boast just two 0.50 in machine guns as armament, and lacked any protective armour or self-sealing tanks. However, combat reports filtering in from Europe proved the folly of a lightweight fighter, and the USAAC modified its design requirements to include an eight-gun fitment, heavy armour plating and a self-sealing fuel system. Republic responded with an all-new design, powered, crucially, by a turbocharged R-2800 Double Wasp radial engine. Despite initial reliability problems with its powerplant, production of the Republic design forged ahead. Although best known for its operational service with the Eighth Air Force, the P-47D was also widely used in the fighter-bomber role in the MTO as well. The first examples arrived in Tunisia just in time to participate in the Allied invasion of Sicily and Italy, and the fighter proved a resounding success. Only the 325th FG flew the Thunderbolt with the Fifteenth Air Force, the unit fulfilling long-range escort duties for B-17 and B-24 bombers striking at Axis strongholds in northern Italy and the Balkans. Equipped with the Thunderbolt for six months, the 325th produced half a dozen P-47 aces in this time. A further five groups saw extended service with the Republic fighter as part of the Twelfth Air Force, although they flew predominantly ground support missions and produced no aces.

P-47D-23 42-75008 *BIG STUD* of Lt Col Robert L Baseler, CO of the 325th FG, Lesina, Italy, April 1944

A larger than life character whose aircraft nickname caught on, Baseler officially scored six kills. He was one of the 325th's early aces, five of his tally being achieved while flying the P-40F over Sardinia between May-July 1943. Having been the first CO of the 319th FS upon its arrival in the MTO in August 1942, Baseler continued to keep his aircraft (firstly a P-40F and then a 'razorback' Thunderbolt) with this unit following his promotion to the 325th FG's HQ flight. The 319th's squadron colour was yellow, hence the trim to the red theatre nose band on 42-75008. A 'bubbletop' P-47 was later painted with similar markings to those shown after Baseler had left the group. Despite leaving the 325th FG on 1 April 1944, Baseler unofficially completed a number of missions in the new Mustang, which the group first flew on operations on 27 May 1944.

NIGHT FIGHTER

'Heinz always preferred to attack the Avro bomber from directly astern, where its exhaust pattern could be seen from a distance of about 2500 ft.'

The leading nightfighter ace of World War 2, Heinz Schnaufer was credited with an astounding 121 victories, all of which were scored during the hours of darkness. The vast majority of these kills consisted of RAF four-engined heavy bombers like the Lancaster, Halifax and Stirling. For almost three years Schnaufer enjoyed unstoppable success in the night skies over occupied Europe. A hugely talented pilot, he was backed in his quest to blunt Bomber Command's near-nightly raids on Germany by his *Bordfunker* (radio operator), Fritz Rumpelhardt, and later his *Bordmechaniker* (Flight Mechanic), Wilhelm Gänsler.

The painting featured in this chapter depicts Schnaufer and his crew in action near the Dutch coast on the evening of 15 February 1944. During the course of a sortie which lasted for two hours and twenty minutes, they succeeded in downing three Lancasters – Schnaufer's 45th, 46th and 47th kills. These bombers were part of a force of 891 aircraft despatched by Bomber Command to strike at Berlin as part of an ongoing campaign specifically targeting the German capital. This proved to be the largest raid ever sent against Berlin, Bomber Command losing 26 Lancasters and 17 Halifaxes to flak and nightfighters.

Bordfunker Rumpelhardt, who now lives in retirement in Kehl, recounted this memorable sortie specially for this volume;

'The night of 15/16 February 1944 was one of great drama for

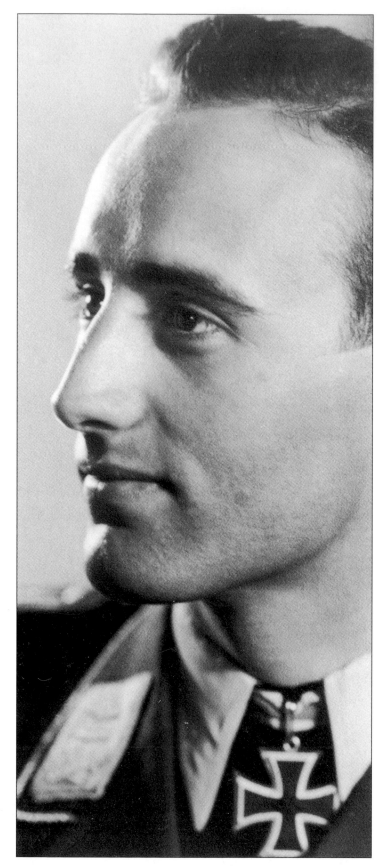

This official photograph was taken of Oberleutnant Schnaufer soon after he was awarded the Knight's Cross on 31 December 1943. Although most pilots received this highly valued decoration after claiming 25 victories, Germany's ranking nightfighter ace had destroyed 42 aircraft by the time his *Ritterkreuz* was promulgated (*via Peter Hinchliffe*)

us. Heinz had had a slight stomach ache all day, but could not resist flying the night's mission once a large formation of British bombers had been reported approaching. So we took off in Bf 110 "G9+EZ" at about 2205 hours and headed for sector "Eisbär" ("Polar bear").

'In intervals of about 15 to 20 minutes, Heinz managed to shoot down three Lancasters: the first (No 103 Sqn Lancaster III ND363/'PM-A') fell into the open sea; the second one (No 115 Sqn Lancaster II LL689/'KO-P') crashed near Hoorn, on the banks of the Ijsselmeer/Zuider Zee, north of Amsterdam; and the third (No 622 Sqn Lancaster I W4272/'GJ-C') fell into the offshore mudflats known as the "Wattenmeer".

'Heinz always preferred to attack the Avro bomber from directly astern, where its exhaust pattern could be seen from a distance of about 2500 ft.

'On the stroke of midnight, the fighter control officer came up on the ground-to-air radio to wish Oberleutnant Heinz Schnaufer, the newly-appointed *Gruppenkommandeur* of IV./NJG 1, a happy 22nd birthday. I added my congratulations too.

'Heinzen's pains were obviously getting worse, and we were more than happy when we landed safely back at Leeuwarden at 0014 hours. A champagne reception was awaiting us at Ops HQ, but it had to take place without the guest of honour. Anybody who knew Heinz – who was never one to miss out on a celebration – realised what the absence meant. His condition must have been serious.

'A birthday party had been arranged for the entire *gruppe* at our local inn after lunch on that day. On my way there, I was told that

The most successful nightfighter crew ever – *Bordmechaniker* (Flight Mechanic) Wilhelm Gänsler, *Flugzeugführer* Heinz Schnaufer and *Bordfunker* Fritz Rumpelhardt. Both Schnaufer and Rumpelhardt had paired up during flight training in mid-1941, whilst Gänsler had joined 'the team' in the autumn of 1943 (*via Peter Hinchliffe*)

Following the engagements of 15 February 1944, Schnaufer points out the freshly-applied 'official' victory markings for his 45th, 46th and 47th kills on the fin of his Bf 110G-4 at St Trond (*via Peter Hinchliffe*)

Heinz was about to have an appendix operation. I dashed to the hospital as if my own life depended upon it, and was just in time to shake Heinz by the hand and wish him all the best as he was being wheeled into the operating theatre.

'The British enjoyed a month-long respite from the attentions of Heinz whilst he recovered from his operation, and we did not claim our next victory until the night of 22/23 March.'

This Bf 110G-4 boasts the large offset dipoles associated with the *Lichtenstein* SN-2 radar, as well as the protruding cannon barrels for the MG 151 20 mm cannon. Note also the flame damper shroud fitted to the exhaust stubs (*via Peter Hinchliffe*)

PILOT BIOGRAPHY – HEINZ SCHNAUFER

Born in the small town of Calw, on the edge of the Black Forest, Heinz-Wolfgang Schnaufer is unquestionably the world's most successful nightfighter pilot, having scored all 121 of his victories between June 1942 and March 1945.

Requesting to join the *Nachtjagd* towards the end of his flight training, the 20-year-old Schnaufer arrived at II./NJG 1 in the spring of 1942. He claimed his first kill on 2 June, and between that date and August 1943, when he was promoted to the command of 12./NJG 1, he added a further 20 victories.

As the RAF's night bombing offensive grew in intensity, the *Nachtjagd* crews found themselves almost overwhelmed by targets, and for a talented pilot like Schnaufer, this translated into numerous multiple-victory missions. For example, on the night of 16 December 1943, despite low cloud and generally poor visibility, he was credited with the destruction of four Lancasters. Thirteen days later, two more Avro heavy bombers fell to his guns, taking his score to 42, and earning the now Oberleutnant Schnaufer the Knight's Cross.

He claimed five Lancasters in just 14 minutes on the night of 25 May, and was awarded the Oak Leaves on 24 June, with his tally standing at 64. The Swords followed just over a month later, and on 9 October 1944 Schnaufer became only the second nightfighter pilot (after Helmut Lent) to achieve 100 kills – for which he was awarded the Diamonds.

He was made *Geschwaderkommodore* of NJG 4 in November, and his greatest achievement as a nightfighter pilot came on 21 February 1945, when he downed two Lancasters in the early hours of the morning, followed by a further seven (in just 17 minutes) that evening.

As with a number of leading German *Experten*, Heinz Schnaufer survived the hostilities only to be killed in a postwar accident. The once-famed 'Night Ghost of St Trond' died in France following a car accident in July 1950.

SPECIFICATION

Messerschmitt Bf 110G
(all dimensions and performance data for Bf 110G-4c/R3)

TYPE:	twin-engined monoplane fighter
ACCOMMODATION:	two-/three-man crew
DIMENSIONS:	length 42 ft 9.75 in (13.09 m) wingspan 53 ft 3.75 in (16.26 m) height 13 ft 8.5 in (4.22 m)
WEIGHTS:	empty 11,220 lb (5089 kg) normal loaded 20,700 lb (9389 kg)
PERFORMANCE:	maximum speed 342 mph (547.2 kmh) range 1305 miles (2088 km) with two external tanks powerplants two Daimler-Benz DB 605B-1 engines output 2950 hp (2199 kW)
ARMAMENT:	two 30 mm cannon in nose cowling, two 20 mm cannon in belly pack, two 7.9 mm machine guns in nose cowling and one 7.9 mm machine gun in rear cockpit
FIRST FLIGHT DATE:	Autumn 1941
OPERATORS:	Germany
PRODUCTION:	approximately 6050 (all models)

When Germany invaded Poland on 1 September 1939, the Luftwaffe's nightfighter force was virtually non-existent thanks to its leader, Reichmarschall Hermann Göring, who boasted that bombs would never fall on Germany. By mid-1940 his folly was evident, and the first nightfighter wing – *Nachtjagdgeschwader* 1 – had been hastily formed with Bf 110s. Messerschmitt's twin-engined heavy fighter would remain in the forefront of the night war over occupied Europe through to VE-Day, despite its virtual removal from the day fighter force a year earlier. The nocturnal mission was ideally suited to a twin-engined, multi-seat fighter like the Bf 110, and Messerschmitt produced a series of aircraft tailored exclusively to the nightfighting role. These began to replace surplus C-models (issued to the *Nachtjagd* in 1940 following their removal from the *Zerstörergeschwader* in the wake of the Battle of Britain debacle) from early 1942 onwards. The Bf 110G was radar-equipped, and accounted for around 60 per cent of the overall *Nachtjagd* force for the final three years of the war. The best nightfighter variant of all the Bf 110s was the G-4, which boasted DB 605B-1 engines, FuG 212 *Lichtenstein* C-1, SN-2 or 221a radar and various cannon fits, depending on the sub-type. So effective was the Bf 110G in this role that the fighter remained in production until March 1945.

Bf 110G-4 'G9+EZ' of Oberleutnant Heinz Schnaufer, *Staffelkapitän* of 12./NJG 1, St Trond, February 1944

Oberleutnant Schnaufer enjoyed success with this Bf 110G-4, fitted with FuG 202 radar, flame damper shrouds, an extended barrel nose cannon and *Schräge Musik*, on at least five occasions in 1943-44 according to his *Bordfunker*, Fritz Rumpelhardt. The aircraft wears typical nightfighter markings for the period, the *Nachtjagd* making less use of colour in regard to *Staffel* letters and so forth than other branches of the Luftwaffe, as high visibility was hardly necessary. Its rudder bears a tally of 47 kills scored by Schnaufer up to that time, his most recent being on the night of the 14 February 1944.

THE LONG REACH

'Never give the Hun an even break. If you have any advantage on him, keep it and use it.'

At 1120 hours on 23 March 1944, P-51 Mustangs from the 4th FG, led by the redoubtable Col Don Blakeslee, rendezvoused at 24,000 ft with B-17 Flying Fortresses from the 3rd Bomb Division west of Hanover. The 'heavies' were heading for Brunswick, and the fighters had been allocated the role of Target Support. A group of P-38 Lightnings were also in the area tasked with the same mission.

As the bombers came into view, Capt Duane 'Bee' Beeson, CO of the 334th FS, immediately spotted 25+ Bf 109s and Fw 190s pressing home their attacks on the beleaguered B-17s. He immediately ordered his squadron to attack, punching off his aircraft's 75-gallon drop tanks and opening the throttle of his P-51B.

A highly experienced fighter ace with 14 kills already to his credit, Capt Beeson's record was so outstanding that he was one of a handful of VIII Fighter Command pilots polled for their combat survival tips. These were subsequently included in the Army Air Force's unofficial fighter training manual, *The Long Reach*, which was published in the autumn of 1944.

'Bee' Beeson certainly made full use of the following hints and tips on 23 March, for he was credited with downing two Bf 109s east of Munster, as well as damaging a train!

'I think that the most important single thing to a fighter pilot is speed! The faster an aircraft is moving when he spots an enemy aircraft, the sooner he will be able to take the bounce and get to the Hun. And it's harder for him to bounce you if you are going fast. Of course, keeping a high speed in formations is very hard

Capt Duane 'Bee' Beeson, CO of the 334th FS, recounts details of his recently completed escort mission to groundcrewmen (out of shot) at Debden in March 1944. Note the 'Bee' emblem on his flying helmet (*via Sam Sox*)

Iain Wyllie

ABOVE Photographed by a grateful bomber crewman, a squadron of P-51Bs from the 4th FG is seen flying Target Support several thousand feet above the 'heavies' as they head for Germany. On the 23 March 1944 mission depicted in the artwork in this chapter, despite the intervention of the 4th FG, some 16 B-17s were lost out of the 224 despatched (*via Michael O'Leary*)

RIGHT Two of the 4th FG's leading aces pose for an official AAF photograph at Debden in early March 1944. Duane Beeson (left) finished the war with 17.33 aerial victories and 4.75 ground kills and Don Gentile (right) was credited with 21.833 aircraft destroyed in the air and 6 on the ground. Both men subsequently died in the immediate postwar years, Beeson of a brain tumour in 1947 and Gentile in a flying accident in 1951 (*via Michael O'Leary*)

BELOW Typical of the P-51B/Cs that equipped the 4th FG in 1944-45, this particular aircraft (43-103603) served with the 336th FS for almost a year (*via Sam Sox*)

because the formation falls apart, and also because of trying to save gas. But it is an important thing for a pilot to remember when he gets separated from his group, or when split up into small units. Also, when actually bouncing a Hun it is good to have as much speed as possible. The aircraft that has speed has the advantage on the one that hasn't. He has the initiative because speed can always be converted into altitude.

'The problem of overshooting a Hun comes up quite often in both the P-47 and the P-51 because of the very high overtaking speed they pick up in the dive. My own idea is that overshooting is a very good thing. Speed is good and should never be lost. When you keep a high speed up you can be sure of closing into range before opening fire, and the closer you get, the better

chance you have of hitting him. Also, another good point to remember is that when you are bouncing a Hun, you are on the offensive and have the advantage. But things happen in split seconds up there, and you don't know what might happen, so that you will suddenly find the same Hun, or one of his friends, back on your tail shooting at you.

'Never give the Hun an even break. If you have any advantage on him, keep it and use it. So, when attacking, I would say plan to overshoot him if possible; hold fire until within range, then shoot and clobber him down to the last instant before breaking away. It's sorta' like sneaking up behind him and hitting him with a baseball bat. When this is done, a pilot will have to be careful not to ram the other aircraft on the breakaway.'

PILOT BIOGRAPHY – DUANE 'BEE' BEESON

Born in Boise, Idaho, on 16 July 1921, Beeson eventually moved to California, where he worked as a hotel clerk. Deciding to leave this boring job behind, he joined the Royal Canadian Air Force on 23 June 1941, and was commissioned as a pilot officer on 26 February 1942, being sent overseas shortly afterwards.

Once in England, Beeson firstly completed the five-month long Spitfire conversion course at RAF Usworth, just south of Newcastle-upon-Tyne, with No 55 Operational Training Unit, before being posted to No 71 'Eagle' Sqn at Debden, in Essex. He arrived on the unit on 5 September, and 24 days later became a part of the US Army Air Force when No 71 Sqn was transferred to VIII Fighter Command control.

Now flying with the 4th Fighter Group (FG), 2Lt Beeson was a assigned to the 334th FS, which swapped its Spitfire VBs for P-47C Thunderbolts in early 1943. He seemed to click with the Republic 'heavyweight', and scored his first victory on 19 May 1943 when he shot down a Bf 109 over Holland. From that point on his score rapidly rose, and he became the 4th FG's first ace on 8 October.

'Bee' Beeson was given command of the 334th FS on 15 March – by which time the unit had converted to P-51B Mustangs. On 5 April 1944, he was shot down by flak while strafing a German airfield at Brandenburg, near Berlin. Immediately taken prisoner, Beeson was released following the surrender of Germany. He elected to stay in the AAF postwar, and was promoted to lieutenant-colonel on 24 October 1945. However, a promising career was cut cruelly short when Duane 'Bee' Beeson died from a brain tumour on 13 February 1947, aged just 25.

SPECIFICATION

North American P-51B-5 Mustang

TYPE:	single-engined monoplane fighter
ACCOMMODATION:	pilot
DIMENSIONS:	length 32 ft 3 in (9.83 m) wingspan 37 ft 0 in (11.28 m) height 13 ft 8 in (4.16 m)
WEIGHTS:	empty 6980 lb (3166.12 kg) maximum take-off 11,800 lb (5352.48 kg)
PERFORMANCE:	maximum speed 439 mph (702.4 kmh) range 2700 miles (4320 km) with external tanks powerplant Packard V-1650-3 output 1380 hp (1019 kW)
ARMAMENT:	six 0.50 in machine guns in wings; up to 2000 lb (907 kg) of bombs or six 5 in (12.7 cm) rocket projectiles under wings
FIRST FLIGHT DATE:	13 October 1942
OPERATORS:	China, UK, USA
PRODUCTION:	1988

Derived from the Allison-engined P-51A Mustang, which had been built in record time to a British requirement for a new fighter type, the Rolls-Royce Merlin-powered P-51B proved a revelation when first flown in October 1942. The original North American design had suffered from poor performance in the high-altitude dogfights that characterised air combat in Europe. However, the airframe itself was more than sound, so the RAF quickly searched for a replacement powerplant and came up with the Merlin 61. Once mated with this battle-proven engine, the aircraft began to realise its full potential as a fighter – a communiqué of the findings was immediately sent to the manufacturer in the USA, and the rest is history. Car builder Packard was granted a licence to build the Merlin as the Packard V-1650, and North American followed the British lead in mating surplus P-51A airframes with the 'new' powerplant. The Merlin-powered P-51B made its combat debut over Europe in December 1943, just when the Eighth Air Force's much-vaunted daylight bombing campaign had begun to falter due to unsustainable losses. Here was their 'knight in shinning armour', capable of escorting B-17s and B-24s throughout their hazardous missions. Soon, the P-51B had proven itself to be the best long-range fighter in the Allied arsenal at that time, and VIII Fighter Command clamoured for additional aircraft to be allocated to its fighter groups. Aside from the 1988 B-models produced by the parent company at its Inglewood, California, plant, an additional 1750 near-identical C-models were also completed in a new factory in Dallas, Texas.

P-51B-5 Mustang 43-6819 *BEE* of Capt Duane W 'Bee' Beeson, CO of the 334th FS/4th FG, Debden, April 1944

One of the first P-51Bs issued to the 4th FG, this aircraft is finished in the standard overall olive drab (OD) over neutral grey undersurfaces which remained in favour until mid-1944. The colours were applied in such a way that they would gradually blend into one another through the use of slight overspray. White recognition stripes were also painted across the wings, tailplane, fin and around the nose, although these were removed during the course of March-April 1944. As with most other P-51Bs in the 4th FG, 43-6819 had its white nose marking oversprayed with red (the 4th FG's colour) in mid-March. The paint had been purchased locally, and the pigment content was so low that groundcrews had to apply up to six coats to fully obscure the white marking beneath it. The white fin and tail bands seen on the aircraft in Iain Wyllie's artwork on the previous spread were immediately painted out upon Beeson's return to Debden in the wake of the 23 March mission. All of 'Bee' Beeson's Mustang kills were claimed in this aircraft, and he was also flying it when shot down by flak on 5 April.

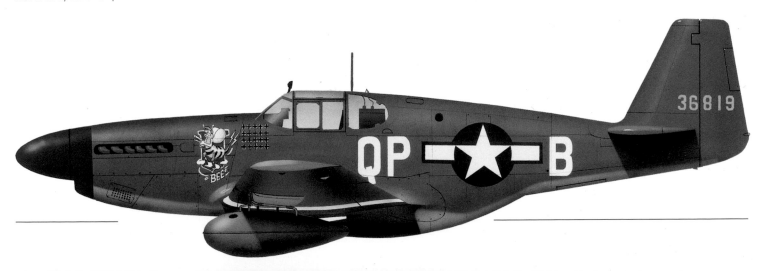

'ILLU'

'I stopped shooting and levelled out 30 ft above the ice. My target crashed into the ice close to Seiskari.'

On 6 March 1944 three Bf 109Gs of 1/HLeLv 34 and six Brewster Model 239s of 3/HLeLv 24 were sent to patrol the eastern end of the Gulf of Finland, with the instruction to await the arrival of Soviet aircraft returning to their bases at Seiskari and Oranienbaum. At 1745 hours, 16 Petlyakov Pe-2 bombers of 12.GBAP, escorted by a dozen fighters, were observed at a distance of one kilometre by the Finnish pilots. They immediately split up, with some fighters going for the bombers, and others for the escorts. Amongst the attacking Finns was WO Ilmari Juutilainen;

'I knew that it was important to spare the ammunition because there were a great many targets. In the growing twilight, the defensive fire of the bombers' rear gunners was clearly visible. It looked like a swarm of fireflies. The fireflies looked very innocent, but when they hit they were very nasty insects!'

The Finnish ace quickly shot down two of the Pe-2s, and had latched onto potentially his third kill when he saw what he thought were two Bf 109s taking position as his wingmen;

'I turned to them and rocked my wings as a sign of attack because they didn't respond to my radio call. One of them came in on my left, the other on my right, and the three of us started to converge.

'I then took my last look around before choosing my next target. Suddenly, I got the feeling that something was wrong. Was there something odd about my wingmen? I looked again and abruptly pulled up into a tight climbing turn, for now I realised that they were my enemies. They were not Messerschmitts at all. They were Yak-7 fighters!

'I had misidentified them as Messerschmitts. I don't know to this day whether they had also misidentified me, because without

1/HLeLv 34's WO Ilmari Juutilainen, photographed on 1 July 1944 at Taipalsaari (*SA-kuva*)

following me, they turned back in the direction from which they came to Seiskari.

'I wiped the sweat from my forehead and started to follow them. The Pe-2s were already too far away and out of reach. I was able to approach my former "section pals" without any trouble though. It was already getting quite dark when I got to a proper range behind the wingman. When I opened fire, the pilot started to turn, then apparently changed his mind and went into a shallow dive from 3500 ft while I followed and hurried him along with long bursts. I stopped shooting and levelled out 30 ft above the ice. My target crashed into the ice close to Seiskari. The other fighter I saw as a distant silhouette as it hurried away.

'All the way home I found myself wondering about the peculiar behaviour of these "faqirs", and still do so today.'

The three kills scored by Ilmari Juutilainen on this sortie took his tally to 61, the last 17 of which had been claimed in Bf 109G-2 MT-222. WO Juutilainen would end the war as Finland's top ace with 94 confirmed and 34 unconfirmed aerial victories.

ABOVE WO Juutilainen's MT-222 (wearing his personal 'Yellow 2' marking above its exhaust stubs) was photographed next to Douglas DC-2 *Hanssin Jukka* at Helsinki-Malmi in late May 1943. The latter aircraft was used to shuttle fighter pilots to Germany to collect Bf 109Gs that were then flown back to Finland (*via Kari Stenman*)

BELOW 'Illu' sits snugly within the cramped confines of MT-222 (Wk-Nr 13528) at Suulajärvi during the summer of 1943. Although not a large man, his shoulders rubbed on the sides of the cockpit in the Bf 109G. Finland's ranking ace scored 17 victories with MT-222 (*via Kari Stenman*)

PILOT BIOGRAPHY – 'ILLU' JUUTILAINEN

Ilmari Juutilainen was born in Lieksa, in eastern Finland, on 21 February 1914. In 1935 he enlisted in the air force, and on 1 May 1937 was posted to LAs. 5 (Air Station 5) as a reconnaissance sergeant pilot. He subsequently retrained as a fighter pilot and was duly posted to the 3rd Flight of LLv 24, which was equipped with D.XXI, on 3 March 1939.

On 30 November 1939 the Winter War broke out, and in his first combat on 19 December 1939, 'Illu' Juutilainen downed a Tupolev SB bomber. He subsequently flew a further 114 missions during the conflict.

With the commencement of the Continuation War on 25 June 1941, Juutilainen saw much action with Brewster Model 239-equipped 3/HLeLv 24. On 26 April 1942 he became the 50th recipient of Finland's highest military decoration, the Mannerheim Cross, for scoring 20 victories. In February of the following year he was posted to 1/HLeLv 34.

At his new unit 'Illu' flew Bf 109G-2s, and he enjoyed such success with the German fighter that by 26 June 1944 his score had increased to 75 kills. Two days later he won the Mannerheim Cross for the second time – he and second-ranking Finnish ace Hans Wind were the first to achieve such an accolade. Indeed, this award was issued twice to just four Finnish soldiers.

In celebration of this rare award, 'Illu' claimed six kills in a single sortie on 30 June. By the time the armistice with the Soviet Union was signed on 3 September 1944, Juutilainen had been credited with 94 victories in 437 missions, making him the highest scoring non-German ace in Europe.

On 16 May 1947 Juutilainen resigned from the air force with a full pension. He bought a light aircraft and became a regular sight at various airshows for a decade until fully retiring. Ilmari 'Illu' Juutilainen passed away on 21 February 1999 – the very day he turned 85.

SPECIFICATION

Messerschmitt Bf 109G
(all dimensions and performance data for Bf 109G-2)

TYPE:	single-engined monoplane fighter
ACCOMMODATION:	pilot
DIMENSIONS:	length 29 ft 7.5 in (9.03 m) wingspan 32 ft 6.5 in (9.92 m) height 8 ft 2.5 in (2.50 m)
WEIGHTS:	empty 5550 lb (2520 kg) maximum take-off 6675 lb (3030 kg)
PERFORMANCE:	maximum speed 397 mph (640 kmh) range 620 miles (998 km) with external tank powerplant Daimler-Benz DB 605A-1 output 1475 hp (1100 kW)
ARMAMENT:	one 20 mm cannon in propeller hub and two 7.92 mm machine guns in upper cowling, wing guns optional; provision for various underfuselage and underwing stores
FIRST FLIGHT DATE:	late summer 1941
OPERATORS:	Bulgaria, Croatia, Finland, Germany, Hungary, Italy, Romania, Slovakia, Switzerland
PRODUCTION:	approximately 23,500 G-models

Finland had continually badgered Germany to supply it with Bf 109s from the first months of World War 2, for it was realised that the Messerschmitt fighter was far superior to anything then operated by the modest-sized air force of this small Scandinavian country. Their persistence finally paid off in late 1942, when Germany agreed to sell them 30 Bf 109G-2s to equip one squadron, and cover any attrition – a contract for these fighters was signed on 1 February 1943. Just over a week prior to contracts being exchanged LeLv 34 was established at Immola on 23 January 1943. The new squadron was intended to be a 'crack outfit' right from the start, and only the best pilots were chosen to serve with it. Those selected were sent to Germany for familiarisation on the Bf 109G, where the Luftwaffe training officer placed in charge of the conversion initially insisted on a full-scale training programme as was taught to ab initio *Jagdflieger*. However, upon seeing the skill of the Finnish pilots, he agreed to a much shorter course! On 9 March 1943 the first 16 Bf 109G-2s left for Finland, followed by a second batch of 14 on 10 May. A total of 162 Bf 109Gs were eventually supplied by the Germans up until the armistice in September 1944, and the Finns made good use of them. Some 663 Soviet aircraft were shot down by pilots flying Bf 109Gs, and in return just 27 Messerschmitts were lost in aerial combat – a kill ratio of 25 to 1.

1/HLeLv 34's MT-222 was used by WO Juutilainen until 10 March 1944, when it was lost whilst being flown by MSgt Lauri Mäittälä. The latter pilot was escorting a high-flying photo-reconnaissance aeroplane at the time when they were bounced by La-5s. As he dived away, Mäittälä almost certainly suffered a failure in his oxygen system, for he lost consciousness. By the time he came round at a lower altitude, his aircraft was plummeting to the ground at high-speed. Mäittälä frantically attempted to pull the fighter out of its dive, but the tailplanes on MT-222 failed and he crashed to his death (*via Kari Stenman*)

Bf 109G-2 (Wk-Nr 14753) MT-212/'Red 2' of WO Ilmari Juutilainen, 1/HLeLv 34, Utti, May 1943

MT-212 was assigned to Juutilainen on 13 March 1943, and 11 days later he scored the first Finnish Messerschmitt victory (a Pe-2) with it. On 2 June fellow LeLv 34 ace Oiva Tuominen (44 kills) ditched the fighter after hitting debris from a Pe-2 he had just shot down. Juutilainen's later mounts were MT-222, MT-426 and MT-457, and he finished as the top Finnish ace on the Bf 109G, scoring 58 victories with the German fighter by war's end.

'HADES RED FLIGHT'

'There was a flash of flame and then the "Tojo" started down and almost immediately exploded. The pilot was blown clear and parachuted down.'

This rare shot of a smiling Maj Tom McGuire was taken on 5 January 1945, and it shows him devoid of his distinctively battered service hat, which was a permanent fixture atop his head when the 'Iron Major' was not flying. He was killed in action just 48 hours after this photograph was taken (*via John Stanaway*)

On 19 May 1944 Capt Tom McGuire, who had been CO of the 431st Fighter Squadron (FS) within the 475th Fighter Group (FG) for just 17 days, was leading 'Hades Red Flight' on bomber escort duty to Jefman Island, north of New Guinea, when he spotted three Ki-43s and a lone Ki-44 near Manokwari. Quickly manoeuvring P-38J-15 *PUDGY III* in behind the 'Tojo', which was trailing the trio of 'Oscars', McGuire hit the Nakajima fighter hard with two accurate bursts of fire. Sensing the imminent explosion of his burning mount, the Japanese pilot wisely took to his parachute, thus giving his American victor his 18th kill. McGuire's combat report for this action read as follows;

'We took off from Hollandia drome at 1120/K, rendezvousing with the bombers off the west of Japen Island. I was leading "Red Flight" of "Hades", and we arrived over the target at 1335/K. Flak was heavy calibre, heavy intensity and accurate, bursting between 14,000 and 18,000 ft.

'At 1340/K we made contact with the enemy, consisting of a flight of one "Tojo" and three probable "Oscars" just west of Manokwari. We dropped tanks and started for them. The Nips were diving from above and to the left and ahead of our formation. We slipped in behind them. Picking out the element leader, I opened fire with a short burst and followed him until he stalled out, going straight up and rolling slightly. I then fired

Iain Wyllie

PUDGY IV was the first P-38L-1 used by Tom McGuire, the aircraft being amongst a batch of factory-fresh Lightnings that were delivered to the 431st's base at Biak in the early autumn of 1944. 'Pudgy' was 'Mac's' nickname for his wife Marilynn (*via John Stanaway*)

Tom McGuire scored four kills in November 1944 whilst leading the 431st FS over the Philippines, downing a 'Tojo', an 'Oscar' and two 'Jacks' in a 12-day period at the start of the month. He is seen here in P-38L-1 44-24155 *PUDGY (V)* soon after claiming his 25th kill – the 'Tojo' downed on 1 November en route to Leyte (*via John Stanaway*)

Undoubtedly one of America's greatest ever aviators, Charles Lindbergh toured the Pacific theatre in 1944, flying a number of missions with various P-38 units, including the 8th and 475th FGs. Indeed, he even managed to down a Japanese aircraft whilst on a patrol with the latter group – an action which resulted in 475th boss Col Charles 'Mac' MacDonald being recalled to the US for three months on disciplinary grounds! Lindbergh is seen here at around that time with Capt Tom McGuire, who astonished other senior officers within the 475th FG with his unseemly taunting of the famed transatlantic pilot during his stay with the group at Biak. Lindbergh, however, took the barbs with good grace, and reportedly set McGuire on his heels a time or two himself (*via John Stanaway*)

another short burst, hitting him in the cockpit. There was a flash of flame and then the "Tojo" started down and almost immediately exploded. The pilot was blown clear and parachuted down.

'I then started down after the others; there were approximately eight enemy aircraft in all. When the bombers called that there were some enemy aircraft near, we returned to them and covered them back to Tydeman Reef, where we left the bombers and returned home, landing at 1600/K.

'The Japs flew standard US formation. "Tojo" had dark camouflage and the pilot seemed experienced.'

Although May 1944 generally proved to be a quiet month for aerial combat in 5th Fighter Command, Hollandia-based Capt McGuire had also destroyed an 'Oscar' just 48 hours prior to claiming his 'Tojo'.

By year-end Thomas B 'Mac' McGuire had become the second-ranking American ace of World War 2, having achieved 38 kills.

However, he was to lose his life in combat on 7 January 1945 whilst flying on an unauthorised fighter sweep which had been specially staged to push his score past leading ace 'Dick' Bong's tally of 40 victories.

A controversial figure who polarised the men that flew with him, McGuire's personality and leadership styles have often been commented on in the decades since his death.

'He was an extremely ambitious man. He worked hard, and that's why he got to be squadron commander. He was more a great leader of men in the air than on the ground, stated McGuire's immediate boss (and third-ranking P-38 ace), Col Charles MacDonald, who commanded the 475th FG for much of the time that 'Mac' was CO of the 431st FS. Another who remarked on the P-38 ace's qualities was 433rd FS pilot Carroll Anderson. 'McGuire was an earthy type of guy who led by example. And although he could be abrasive and caustic, he fought and led from the front'.

PILOT BIOGRAPHY – THOMAS 'MAC' McGUIRE

Born in Ridgewood, New Jersey, in August 1920, McGuire entered the Georgia School of Technology in 1937, where he studied mechanical engineering. His interest in aviation first surfaced in 1940 when he learned to fly the Piper Cub at Candler Field, in Florida. McGuire then decided that military flying was for him, and he dropped out of school in July 1941 and enlisted in the army as an aviation cadet.

He completed his training in Texas, and was posted to the 50th Pursuit Group's 313th Pursuit Squadron at Key Field, Mississippi, in early 1942. Flying antiquated P-35s, he asked for overseas duty and was sent to P-39F-equipped 56th PS/54th PG in the Aleutians. Weather was the greatest enemy that fighter pilots faced in this 'forgotten' theatre, and McGuire soon wanted out. Returning to the USA, he converted onto the P-38 and was sent to the 9th FS/49th FG in March 1943. 'Mac' failed to score whilst flying with this group, and it was not until he transferred to the 431st FS/475th FG that he began to make his mark. He claimed his first victories on 18 August over Wewak, and by the end of the year his tally had raced to 16 destroyed.

On 2 May 1944, now Capt Tom McGuire was made CO of the 431st FS. It was whilst leading this high-scoring unit that he kept pace with the ever increasing tally of ranking American ace 'Dick' Bong, the two P-38 pilots enjoying a healthy rivalry up until the latter completed his Pacific tour and rotated home in mid-December. Within days of Bong's departure, McGuire also left the 431st to become the 475th FG's Operations Officer.

He was killed attempting to shoot down his 39th victory on 7 January 1945. Thomas Buchanan McGuire was posthumously awarded the Congressional Medal of Honor in March 1946.

SPECIFICATION

Lockheed P-38J-15 Lighting

TYPE:	twin-engined monoplane fighter
ACCOMMODATION:	pilot
DIMENSIONS:	length 37 ft 10 in (11.53 m) wingspan 52 ft 0 in (15.85 m) height 9 ft 10 in (3.00 m)
WEIGHTS:	empty 12,780 lb (5797 kg) maximum take-off 21,600 lb (9798 kg)
PERFORMANCE:	maximum speed 414 mph (666 kmh) range 2260 miles (3637 km) with external tanks powerplants two Allison V-1710-89/-91 engines output 2850 hp (2126 kW)
ARMAMENT:	one 20 mm cannon and four 0.50 in machine guns in nose; maximum bomb load of 4000 lb (1814 kg) under wings
FIRST FLIGHT DATE:	27 January 1939 (XP-38)
OPERATORS:	USA
PRODUCTION:	2970

From the time of its introduction into combat in mid 1942, the P-38 Lightning was the most successful twin-engined single-seat fighter of World War 2. The vast majority of its many victories were achieved in the Pacific and China-Burma-India (CBI) theatres, despite Lockheed's production delivery priorities being granted to AAF units in Europe in the spirit of the 'Defeat Germany First' policy. There were never more than 15 squadrons of P-38s in the South and South-west Pacific at any one time, and the CBI used only four squadrons, two of which saw most of the action experienced by the fighter. The Far East Air Forces (comprising the Fifth and Thirteenth Air Forces) had to make do with just a precious few Lightnings until the advent of the European invasion in mid-1944 released enough of these unique fighters to satisfy operational needs. The speed, range and firepower of the P-38 made it the fighter of choice for most AAF pilots fighting in the Solomons, New Guinea and the Philippines. Over 1800 Japanese aircraft fell to the guns of P-38s from the Fifth, Seventh and Thirteenth Air Forces in the Pacific and the Tenth and Fourteenth Air Forces in China and Burma, and at war's end surviving Japanese pilots gave grudging tribute to the P-38 as one of their most formidable foes. More than 100 pilots scored at least five aerial victories in the P-38 in the Pacific and CBI, the top American aces of the war flying the aircraft with both confidence and a certain affection which sometimes approached fanatical devotion.

P-38J-15 serial unknown/*PUDGY III* of Maj Tom McGuire, CO of the 431st FS/475th FG, Hollandia, May 1944

This machine was McGuire's mount during the first half of 1944, and it is believed that he scored at least two victories in it – an 'Oscar' on 17 May over Noemfoor Island and a 'Tojo' just 48 hours later near Manokwari, New Guinea. Despite the P-38 ace being severe in the use of his aircraft, *PUDGY III* enjoyed an unusually long service life of around six months (late January through to early July 1944). *PUDGY IV* and *(V)* were not so fortunate, being used up between July and December 1944.

BETTY JANE

'I think the Mustang probably won the war because it had the range as well as the performance, so we could go anywhere that the bombers went.'

Col Charles M 'Sandy' McCorkle turns his personalised P-51B-10 Mustang *Betty Jane* in towards a pair of Ju 88s attempting to stem the Allied push up through Italy in June 1944. Already a Spitfire Mk VIII ace with the 31st FG by this stage of the war, the 'scrappy' McCorkle went on to claim another six kills whilst flying Mustangs with the Fifteenth Air Force.

As previously described in this volume, North American's superlative fighter was widely adored by all pilots who got to fly it in combat. The Mustang boasted an outstanding top speed, performed well either at altitude or on the deck, was highly manoeuvrable and allowed an average pilot to gain the ascendancy over an opponent flying virtually any other piston-engined fighter (both Allied and Axis) then in frontline service.

One of those to 'click' with the Mustang was veteran 'Eagle Squadron' pilot (and 14-kill ace) Maj Jim Goodson, who stated in his autobiography, *Tumult in the Clouds*;

'I think the Mustang probably won the war because it had the range as well as the performance, so we could go anywhere that the bombers went. The P-51 was a most remarkable plane, but it wasn't as much fun to fly as the Spit. The Mustang was not quite

A veteran of 110 combat missions by the time this shot was taken in June 1944 at San Severo by an official AAF photographer, Col Charles McCorkle was nearing the end of his frontline tour in command of the 31st FG. He is seen seated in his personal P-51B-10 42-106501, which he christened *Betty Jane* (*via Paul Ludwig*)

as tight in the turn, but it was faster than the Spitfire or the Fw 190 or the Bf 109, and of course it had this remarkable range, but it could also turn pretty well. I've out-turned a Fw 190 in a Mustang, but more importantly the P-51 had superior performance from 30,000 ft down to the deck, and could do this 750 miles from home. When Göring saw Mustangs escorting the bombers to Berlin, he knew the war was over.'

Even aces who scored the bulk of their kills on other types placed the Merlin-engined P-51 at the top of the pile. One such pilot was legendary 56th FG boss, Col Hubert 'Hub' Zemke, who claimed just 2.5 kills out of a total of 17.75 victories in the Mustang;

'By far the best air-to-air fighter in the USAAF below 25,000 ft, the P-51D had a very good radius of action for the type of work we did in Europe. The acceleration from slow cruise to maximum performance was excellent compared with that of the competition. Its rate of roll was good and it manoeuvred easily to a learned hand. Dive and acceleration were rapid. Visibility in all directions was ample.

'As an instrument flying aircraft the P-51 was a bit touchy, and it could easily be over-controlled in turbulence. On the question of armament, it carried sufficient machine-guns. Why I say this is that after viewing numerous combat films where pilots fired at extreme range or over-deflected, I came firmly to the conclusion that one should fight for a combat position of ten degrees or less deflection. At close range – 250 yards or less – there is no doubt what would happen when the trigger was depressed: it was a matter of ducking the flying pieces after that.'

Perhaps the final word on the Mustang in the ETO/MTO should go to 18.5-kill ace Maj Leonard 'Kit' Carson. He completed two combat tours in the P-51 with the 357th FG, claimed five Fw 190 victories in one mission and even succeeded in damaging three Me 262s during fleeting aerial engagements in the final weeks of the war. Upon completing his first flight in the Mustang Carson exclaimed, 'You've got a horse-and-a-half here m'boy'.

This P-51B-10 was assigned to the 307th FS at the time Col McCorkle headed the 31st FG. One of the first Mustangs issued to the group, it has the famous red nose and tail-striping associated with the 31st FG during its P-51-period (*via Paul Ludwig*)

Col McCorkle receives an award from Brig-Gen Dean C Strother, commander of the 306th Fighter Wing (which controlled the 31st FG), at San Severo in late 1943. By the end of his 30-year career in the air force, McCorkle had been awarded a Silver Star, the Legion of Merit, the DFC and 23 Air Medals (*via Paul Ludwig*)

Fitted with long-range tanks, a P-51B-10 of the 308th FS departs San Severo at the start of yet another bomber escort mission (*via Paul Ludwig*)

SPECIFICATION

North American P-51B-5 Mustang

TYPE:	single-engined monoplane fighter
ACCOMMODATION:	pilot
DIMENSIONS:	length 32 ft 3 in (9.83 m)
	wingspan 37 ft 0 in (11.28 m)
	height 13 ft 8 in (4.16 m)
WEIGHTS:	empty 6980 lb (3166.12 kg)
	maximum take-off 11,800 lb (5352.48 kg)
PERFORMANCE:	maximum speed 439 mph (702.4 kmh)
	range 2700 miles (4320 km) with external tanks
	powerplant Packard V-1650-3
	output 1380 hp (1019 kW)
ARMAMENT:	six 0.50 in machine guns in wings; up to 2000 lb (907 kg) of bombs or six 5 in (12.7 cm) rocket projectiles under wings
FIRST FLIGHT DATE:	13 October 1942
OPERATORS:	China, UK, USA
PRODUCTION:	1988

PILOT BIOGRAPHY – CHARLES 'SANDY' McCORKLE

A graduate of the army's prestigious West Point Military Academy, Charles McCorkle was commissioned a second lieutenant in the field artillery in June 1936. He soon decided on a career in aviation, however, for he was rated a pilot at Kelly Field, Texas, in early October of that same year! McCorkle transferred to the Army Air Corps exactly 12 months later, and over the next five years accrued much experience serving as both a fighter pilot and an instructor.

In June 1942 he was posted to the 54th FG in Alaska, which was embroiled in the fight for the Aleutians at the time. Flying P-39s, McCorkle was given command of the group three months after his arrival in-theatre, and he subsequently led the outfit back to the USA at the end of 1942. In the spring of the following year the 54th FG became the first AAF group to receive P-51B Mustangs, after which its trio of squadrons were redesignated replacement training units.

By now a full colonel, McCorkle was transferred to the MTO in August 1943 to oversee the transition of the 31st FG onto the North American fighter. This group had been flying the Spitfire since its arrival in Europe in the autumn of 1942, and with Mustangs not available until March 1944, its new CO would get ample opportunity to become familiar with the superlative British fighter. McCorkle had 'made ace' by early February, and he continued to claim victories with the P-51B until he completed his tour in July 1944.

'Sandy' McCorkle remained in the air force postwar, rising to the rank of major-general by the time he retired in 1966.

Four groups operated P-51B/Cs within the recently-formed Fifteenth Air Force from March 1944 through to the early spring of 1945. The Spitfire-equipped 31st and 52nd FGs became the first groups to receive examples of the North American fighter, followed by the 325th and 332nd FGs, both of which gave up P-47Ds. The aircraft soon made its presence felt in the MTO, for on 21 April the 31st FG claimed 17 enemy aircraft destroyed while escorting heavy bombers sent to bomb the oilfields at Ploesti, in Romania. Perhaps the aircraft's single most outstanding achievement came on 31 August when the 52nd FG attacked the Luftwaffe airfield at Reghin, again in Romania, and destroyed over 150 aircraft in an orgy of destruction. Serving primarily as bomber escorts for the burgeoning ranks of B-17 and B-24 'heavies' tasked with knocking out strategic targets in Germany, Austria and the Balkans, pilots within the four Mustang groups saw plenty of action – indeed, no fewer than 50 of them achieved sufficient kills to be classified as aces. By early 1945 most 'razorback' P-51B/Cs had been replaced by the definitive P-51D/K, and the North American fighter remained a familiar sight in southern European skies until VE-Day.

P-51B-10 42-106501 *Betty Jane* of Col Charles M McCorkle, CO of the 31st FG, San Severo, Italy, June 1944

It was the group CO's prerogative to use his own initials instead of a conventional three-letter code, thus McCorkle had the codes 'CM-M' painted on his aircraft, repeating the letters 'CM' on the nose. The 31st FG otherwise used the same codes as the 78th FG in Britain, which was a deliberate duplication aimed at confusing the enemy. The group initially adorned its aircraft with a single diagonal red stripe as its distinguishing marking, before five parallel diagonal stripes, covering the entire tailfin, rudder and tailplanes, took its place. McCorkle was already an ace when the 31st replaced its much-loved Spitfires Mk VIIIs with Mustangs, the colonel subsequently adding six P-51 kills to the five he had previously scored flying the British fighter.

DZIUBEK

'I dived down on them and gave one a three-second burst, after which he caught fire and went straight into the sea.'

During the summer of 1944, the Polish-manned No 315 Sqn used the extensive range of its Mustang IIIs to roam across occupied Europe from Normandy to Norway. Based at Brenzett, in Kent, the unit was led by veteran Spitfire ace Sqn Ldr Eugeniusz *Dziubek* Horbaczewski, who had fought the Luftwaffe with the Polish and French air forces prior to joining the RAF.

One of the most successful long-range missions flown by the unit took place on 30 July 1944, when six Mustang IIIs downed eight German fighters off the Norwegian coast. Horbaczewski's report from that combat read as follows;

'While escorting Beaufighters over the Norwegian coast on July 30th at 1555 hrs, we met about 15 ME 109s and attacked them. We were above them and the MEs were apparently not expecting to see single-engined fighters so far north, as they took no evasive action, possibly mistaking us for other ME 109s. I dived down on them and gave one a three-second burst, after which he caught fire and went straight into the sea. I climbed up, and when climbing I spotted another ME 109 below me. I came down and gave him a long burst. Strikes were seen in the cockpit and on the wings, glycol began to leak from the enemy aircraft, and it was losing speed and height. My guns jammed so I formated on him and started calling by R/T my No 2 (Flg Off Bozydar Nowosielski). The enemy aircraft had no hood and I could see that the pilot's face was covered in blood, and he put up his hands.

'He was heading towards the Norwegian coast, so I ordered my No 2 to open fire. After two bursts, my No 2 overshot him, and the enemy aircraft went into the sea. When last seen, the pilot was adjusting his Mae West. I claim 1¹/₂ ME 109s destroyed.'

Also involved in this action was Flt Lt Michal Cwynar, who 'made ace' during the course of the engagement. He later recalled;

Sqn Ldr Horbaczewski poses alongside his No 315 Sqn Mustang III FB387/'PK-G' at Brenzett. The distinctive unit badge and a fraction of his impressive combat tally can be seen adorning his fighter. When this photograph was taken in early August 1944, Horbaczewski's Mustang III boasted 13¹/₂ crosses and four V1 kill markings (*Bozydar Nowosielski archive*)

Iain Wyllie

'One of Horbaczewski's wingmen spotted German fighters approaching through a fjord's inlet, heading for the Beaufighters. There were two groups of four Bf 109s leisurely, almost nonchalantly, carrying out a left-hand turn in order to take up position to attack the Canadians. Jettisoning our wing fuel tanks, we attacked. Horbaczewski went in first, attacking the inner group, and I engaged the outer formation.

'In diving and then climbing in a left-hand turn, I had engaged the group's leader. By the way he was scything through the air, the edges of his Messerschmitt's wings stitching the sky with air-condensed threads, I realised he was good. He pulled hard – so did I! With the fuselage fuel tank still full and the Mustang's adverse lateral stability, there wasn't much room for imaginative manoeuvring, so I had to hold a steady, smooth turn. With a few hundred revs always in reserve, I held on patiently. For one 360° circle or more there was stalemate. Then I lowered flaps 10° and was gaining on him.

'My solar plexus stopped churning as I felt sure of getting on his tail, all the time thinking "Pull smoothly. Get that extra reserve throttle on". I got him in my gunsight's illuminated ring, pulled straight through his line of flight, one diameter . . . two . . . three diameters of deflection and then pressed the firing button. For a split second there was nothing, then I saw bullets punching holes, first on his tail section, and then across the fuselage, canopy and the wings . . .'

Groundcrewmen from No 315 Sqn pause to have their photograph taken whilst readying Sqn Ldr Horbaczewski's Mustang III FB166 at Coolham Air Landing Ground, north of Brighton, on 18 June 1944 (*Jerzy B Cynk archives*)

No 315 Sqn pilots pose at Brenzett after the mission to Norway on 30 July 1944 that had seen five of them claim seven German fighters destroyed. They are, from left to right, Plt Off Swistun, Sqn Ldr Horbaczewski, Flg Off Nowosielski, Flt Lt Cwynar and Flt Sgts Jankowski and Bedkowski. Note that Horbaczewski is wearing an American-style life vest, rather than the more bulky RAF type worn by the others. He probably 'acquired' it at the party held by the Eighth Air Force's 4th FG at Debden in April 1944 – fellow-Pole Maj 'Mike' Sobanski was flying with the 4th FG at that time (*Sqn Ldr Michal Cwynar archive*)

A No 315 Sqn Mustang III is seen escorting a No 489 Sqn Beaufighter X across the North Sea during 1944. The Polish unit continued to fly these long-range 'Roadstead' missions to Norway until early 1945 (*via Wojtek Matusiak*)

SPECIFICATION

North American Mustang III

TYPE:	single-engined monoplane fighter
ACCOMMODATION:	pilot
DIMENSIONS:	length 32 ft 3 in (9.83 m)
	wingspan 37 ft 0 in (11.28 m)
	height 13 ft 8 in (4.16 m)
WEIGHTS:	empty 6980 lb (3166.12 kg)
	maximum take-off 11,800 lb (5352.48 kg)
PERFORMANCE.	maximum speed 439 mph (702.4 kmh)
	range 2700 miles (4320 km) with external tanks
	powerplant Packard V-1650-3
	output 1380 hp (1019 kW)
ARMAMENT:	six 0.50 in machine guns in wings; up to 2000 lb (907 kg) bombs or six 5 in (12.7 cm) rocket projectiles under wings
FIRST FLIGHT DATE:	13 October 1942
OPERATORS:	China, UK, USA
PRODUCTION:	770+ Mustang IIIs supplied to the RAF through lend-lcase

PILOT BIOGRAPHY – *DZIUBEK* HORBACZEWSKI

Eugeniusz Horbaczewski was born in 1917 in Kiev. He was known throughout his life as *Dziubek* (an informal Polish word which in English means 'darling' or 'kid'). He joined the air force flying school at Deblin in 1938, and was commissioned in the 13th Promotion on 1 September 1939.

Upon reaching France, Horbaczewski apparently flew with a Polish flight at Bordeaux before fleeing once again to Britain in June 1940 and obtaining a posting to No 303 Sqn. Always ready for action, he was a tough subordinate, and in September 1942 Sqn Ldr Jan Zumbach had him posted away to No 302 Sqn following a series of minor incidents which eventually resulted in a Spitfire being written off. Apparently it was then that *Dziubek* swore he would exceed Zumbach's score!

Horbaczewski then joined the Spitfire-equipped Polish Fighting Team in North Africa, and in six months scored eight kills. Whilst in the MTO he rose through the ranks from flying officer to squadron leader, and was eventually given command of No 43 Sqn.

Upon returning to Britain, Horbaczewski was made OC No 315 Sqn within No 133 Wing, which was led by ranking Polish ace Stanislaw Skalski. Ironically, in mid-1944 *Dziubek* found himself under the command of Jan Zumbach once again after the latter replaced Skalski as Wing Leader – further irony was provided when Horbaczewski finally fulfilled his oath soon after the command change.

Dziubek was killed on 18 August 1944 during an air battle which saw his squadron credited with 16 Fw 190s destroyed – he downed three of them prior to his death. He was unwell that day, and some witnesses claim that he knew he would not survive an encounter with German fighters.

Early RAF Mustang operations had seen the aircraft restricted to fighter-reconnaissance and army co-operation duties due to the poor altitude performance of the fighter's Allison engine. Some 800+ Mk I/IA/IIs had been supplied to the air force in 1941/42, and they remained in service until war's end. The mating of the Merlin engine with the airframe in late 1942 resulted in the production of the P-51B/C for the AAF and the Mustang III for the RAF. The first examples of the revitalised North American fighter were issued to No 19 Sqn in February 1944, and by VE-Day no fewer than 18 ETO-based units had re-equipped with the Mustang III. Six squadrons also saw considerable action with the fighter in the MTO during the final year of the war. Many of the units serving in the ETO were assigned to the 2nd Tactical Air Force for much of 1944, during which time they escorted bombers operating in support of the D-Day invasion of France and flew close-support missions for troops on the ground. The Mustang III also exacted a heavy toll on the pilotless V1 'Doodlebugs' fired against south-east England in mid-1944 – the aircraft was credited with the destruction of 232 flying bombs. By this stage in the war, few manned German aircraft were being encountered in the areas in which the Mustang III operated, but seven pilots nevertheless scored five or more kills in the fighter. The Mk III was slowly replaced in frontline service by the P-51D/K-derived Mk IV from late 1944 onwards.

Mustang III FB166/PK-G of Sqn Ldr Eugeniusz *Dziubek* Horbaczewski, OC No 315 Sqn, Brenzett, June 1944

This aircraft had been ferried from Aston Down to No 315 Sqn by Sgt Tamowicz on 13 April 1944, and subsequently became Horbaczewski's personal mount. On 12 June *Dziubek* flew the Mustang on a successful sortie fresh from an inspection at the Coolham-based No 411 (Polish) Repair & Salvage Unit (RSU), claiming an Fw 190 destroyed before being hit by flak. He then flew the fighter directly back to No 411 RSU for repairs to be effected! FB166 was soon back with No 315 Sqn,

and on 30 July Horbaczewski enjoyed more success with it off the Norwegian coast. Following its eventful spell in the frontline, the Mustang III then spent time with No 61 OTU at Rednal in early 1945, before being allocated to Polish-manned No 316 Sqn at Andrews Field, in Essex, in the last weeks of the war. FB166 was finally struck off charge in December 1946.

'STURMBOCK'

'We undertake that, on every sortie resulting in contact with four-engined bombers, we shall press home the attack to the shortest range.'

By the spring of 1944, the Eighth Air Force's daylight bombing campaign was well and truly in full swing. Hundreds of heavy bombers were venturing deep into occupied Europe, escorted by ever increasing numbers of Mustangs, Thunderbolts and Lightnings. The beleaguered *Jagdwaffe* realised that a single knock-out blow had to be dealt to the massed ranks of Liberators and Fortresses now darkening the skies of the Fatherland.

In an act of true desperation, IV.(*Sturm*)/JG 3 was formed as a dedicated *Sturmgruppe* tasked with implementing new tactics devised to maximise Allied bomber losses. All 68 pilots who volunteered to serve with the unit would be trained to close with the enemy and engage him in 'hand-to-hand', close-quarter, combat. In the air, this translated into heavily armed and armoured Fw 190s attacking the bombers from the front and the rear in tight arrowhead formation, closing right in until a kill was assured. Only as a last resort, and in exceptional circumstances (if the fighter, despite its additional armour, was mortally damaged, for example) would a pilot be expected to ram the enemy, and then only if he had a chance to escape by parachute.

The exhaustive training of IV.(*Sturm*)/JG 3 was nearing completion at the end of May 1944 when its *Gruppenkommandeur*, Hauptmann Wilhelm Moritz, conducted a ceremony at the unit's Salzwedel base at which the following *Sturmgruppe* oath was read out aloud by all those present;

'We swear to fight in Defence of the Reich true to the principles and rules of engagement of the *Sturmgruppe*. We know that, as pilots of the *Sturmgruppe*, we are called upon in a special way to protect and defend to the utmost of our ability the population of our Homeland.

Among IV.(*Sturm*)/JG 3's most experienced pilots was Unteroffizier Willi Maximowitz, who had been in the second group of volunteer pilots to join *Sturmstaffel* 1 when it first formed in the winter of 1943-44. Note the shortened barrel of the starboard MK 108 30 mm cannon, squeezed into the outer gun bay of Maximowitz's *'Sturmbock'* (*via John Weal*)

ABOVE Formation take-off from Schongau in the summer of 1944. Hauptmann Wilhelm Moritz's Fw 190A-8/R8 (Wk-Nr 681382) 'Double Chevron', on the right, kicks up dust as it taxies forward to lead IV.(*Sturm*)/JG 3 into action (*via John Weal*)

BELOW With a groundcrewman guiding him off his right wingtip, Maximowitz carefully taxies 'Black 8' towards the grass strip at Schongau. Like all piston-engined 'taildraggers', visibility over the nose of the Fw 190A-8/R8 was limited to say the least (*via John Weal*)

'We undertake that, on every sortie resulting in contact with four-engined bombers, we shall press home the attack to the shortest range and – if unsuccessful in shooting down the enemy by gunfire – we will destroy him by ramming.'

In practice, relatively few pilots were forced to resort to this ultimate desperate measure, and of those who did, at least 50 per cent were reported to have escaped uninjured by parachute.

The *Gruppe's* favourite tactic was to attack from the rear, each *Staffel* - in broad arrowhead formation – targeting a selected squadron of bombers and slowly overhauling it, holding fire until the very last moment when the signal to do so would be given by the *Staffelführer*. Occasionally, frontal attacks would also be mounted. These were less popular with *Sturmstaffel* pilots as only

the leader, at the tip of the arrowhead, would have the opportunity to line up on a target with any accuracy in the split-second such head-on tactics allowed. The aircraft on either flank had very little time, or room, for any manoeuvring, and often had simply to fire at whatever happened to lay in their path - be it only a wingtip, or even, the cruellest of luck, nothing but the narrow channel of empty space separating two of the closely formated 'heavies'!

One of IV.(*Sturm*)/JG 3's original members, and more successful *Experten*, was Unteroffizier Willi Maximowitz, whose *'Sturmbock'* is depicted in this artwork during a classic 'twelve-o'clock high' frontal attack on a formation of 93rd BG B-24Js over western Germany in the summer of 1944.

PILOT BIOGRAPHY – WILLI MAXIMOWITZ

Unlike the other famous and highly decorated Luftwaffe fighter aces so vividly portrayed in Iain Wyllie's dramatic artwork within this volume, Willi Maximowitz remains a shadowy and virtually unsung figure. His inclusion serves to represent that solid core of NCO pilots – many of them veterans of long years' standing – who provided the backbone of the wartime *Jagdwaffe*, and who contributed so much to their units' successes.

Little is known of Maximowitz's operational career, if any, prior to his service as a *Sturm* pilot. Although not among the 18 original pilots who formed *Sturmstaffel 1* in November 1943, he was one of the second intake of volunteers who joined the unit a few weeks later. Unteroffizier Maximowitz's first victory – a B-24 brought down on 30 January 1944 – was the result of just such an action. He would score three more kills, all B-17s, before the pioneering *Sturmstaffel* was absorbed into IV. (*Sturm*)/JG 3 in the late spring of 1944.

Flying with the *Gruppe's* 11. *Staffel*, Maximowitz added seven more 'heavies' to his total, but was then severely injured when his 'Sturmbock' overturned on landing on 30 July. He returned to operations in late September, now as a *Schwarmführer* (leader of a four-aircraft section) in 14. *Staffel*. Before the year was out, his tally had risen to 15.

Early in 1945 IV.(*Sturm*)/JG 3 was transferred to the Eastern Front, and Feldwebel Maximowitz's last dozen kills were all Russian. A recipient of the German Cross in Gold (an award which ranked just below the Knight's Cross), Maximowitz and his entire *Schwarm* were reported missing after last being seen under attack by Soviet fighters east of Berlin on 20 April 1945.

SPECIFICATION

Focke-Wulf Fw 190A-8

TYPE:	single-engined monoplane fighter
ACCOMMODATION:	pilot
DIMENSIONS:	length 29 ft 4.25 in (8.95 m)
	wingspan 34 ft 5.5 in (10.50 m)
	height 12 ft 11.5 in (3.95 m)
WEIGHTS:	empty 7650 lb (3470 kg)
	maximum take-off 9656 lb (4380 kg)
PERFORMANCE:	maximum speed 402 mph (647 kmh)
	range 643 miles (1035 km)
	powerplant BMW 801D-2
	output 1700 hp (1268 kW)
ARMAMENT:	two 7.9 mm machine guns in nose, four 20 mm cannon in wings (A-8/R8 'Sturmbock' had outer 20 mm cannon replaced with 30 mm cannon)
FIRST FLIGHT DATE:	1 June 1939
OPERATORS:	Germany
PRODUCTION:	1334

The final production A-series Fw 190, the A-8 featured a new radio, repositioned fuselage bomb rack and space for an internal auxiliary fuel tank. As with previous models of the Focke-Wulf fighter, myriad *Umrüst-Bausätze* (factory conversion sets) and *Rüstsätze* (field conversion sets) enabled the basic A-8 to be modified for specialist roles such as bomber attack, ground attack and *Wilde Sau* nightfighting. The A-8 also formed the basis for the 'Sturmbock' ('Battering Ram'), which equipped IV.(*Sturm*)/JG 3 in the spring of 1944. This aircraft featured both additional armour-plating around the cockpit and ammunition boxes and extra panels of laminated glass on the sides of the canopy in an effort to protect the pilot from the bombers' heavy calibre machine gun fire. The A-8/R8 also packed a hefty punch, with single MK 108 30 mm cannon being fitted in the outer wing stations in place of the standard MG 151 20 mm weapons. The former's high-explosive shells proved extremely destructive at short range, with combat experience showing that, on average, a heavy bomber could be brought down with just three 30 mm rounds. The heavy weight of the cannon and the additional armour plating made the 'Sturmbock' far less agile than a standard A-8, however, and when engaged by escorting American fighters the *Sturm* pilot had little chance to defend himself.

Maximowitz's 'Sturmbock' carries JG 3's 'Winged U' badge on the cowling and a IV.*Gruppe* wavy bar on the aft fuselage band. The muzzle of the heavy 30 mm cannon may also be seen outboard of the mainwheel leg (*via John Weal*)

Fw 190A-8/R8 'Black 8' of Unteroffizier Willi Maximowitz, IV.(*Sturm*)/JG 3, Salzwedel, circa June 1944
Unlike the majority of the anonymous A-8/R8s flown by this specialist unit, Willi Maximowitz's 'Sturmböck' featured JG 3's 'Winged U' badge and the IV.*Gruppe* wavy bar marking. 'Black 8' was reportedly one of the aircraft deployed briefly to Normandy. If this is

the case, and in view of its gaudy paint scheme, both it and Maximowitz were lucky to survive! A member of the original *Sturmstaffel 1*, Maximowitz's final tally is uncertain, one source quoting 25 kills, 15 of which were 'heavies' (several destroyed by ramming). He failed to return from an Eastern Front sortie on 20 April 1945.

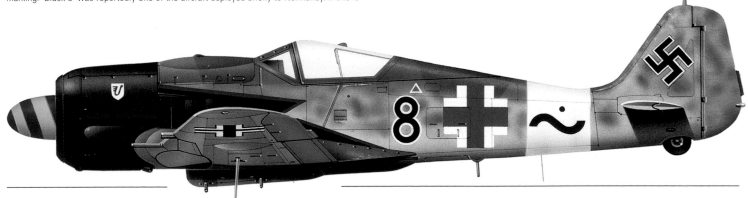

SLOVAKIAN SPITFIRE SUCCESS

'In short, the Spitfire Mk IX was the best fighting aeroplane of its day.'

Much of the fighter offensive conducted by the RAF against 'Fortress Europe' was undertaken by the myriad 'foreign' squadrons that had been hastily established both during and after the Battle of Britain. Polish, Czechoslovakian, French, Norwegian, Dutch and Belgian units flew from the same airfields as long-established Fighter Command squadrons and units manned by pilots from the dominions – Australia, South Africa, Rhodesia, Canada and New Zealand.

Fuelled by a near-fanatical zeal to rid their occupied countries of German forces, foreign fighter pilots sought to engage the enemy whenever possible. Many achieved ace status, and rose to command not only units manned by their fellow countrymen in exile, but also RAF squadrons as well. One such individual was Georgian-born Slovakian ace Otto Smik, who reached Fighter Command's No 11 Group in late 1942 and embarked on a scoring spree that would see him claim ten kills whilst flying with three different units during a two-year spell in the frontline.

Like most other RAF fighter aces of this period, Smik's mount was the superlative Spitfire Mk IX. Arguably the best Merlin-engined version of Supermarine's legendary fighter, the Mk IX had been introduced on the Channel Front just as the Slovakian pilot was finishing his conversion training, prior to being posted to a frontline unit. Both novice pilots like Smik and veteran aces of the calibre of Wg Cdr Al Deere, then Wing Leader at RAF Biggin

Hill, enjoyed great success with the Mk IX. And although the Slovakian's thoughts on the Spitfire were sadly never committed to paper, New Zealander Deere was most effusive about the Mk IX when he penned the foreword for the author's *Spitfire - Flying Legend* volume, published by Osprey in 1996;

'Which was the supreme mark of the Spitfire? There is disagreement among fighter pilots on this issue, but for me the Spitfire LF Mk IXC takes the prize, embodying as it did the attributes of increased power and a greatly improved rate of climb, without in anyway destroying the handling capabilities – always a fine balance between power and manoeuvrability at all levels. Certainly the introduction of the LF IXC in 1943 tilted the balance between the two main combatants. On the German side the formidable Fw 190 had ruled the roost for the past year, and whilst the Spitfire F Mk IXB then in service disputed this supremacy, it was the later IXC with the Merlin 66 engine which eventually occupied the perch, and held onto it until victory was achieved.'

Another ace to reap the benefits of the improved Spitfire during the course of 1943 was then Kenley-based Canadian Wing Leader, Wg Cdr J E 'Johnnie' Johnson;

ABOVE No 222 'Natal' Sqn pilots pose informally in front of one of their Spitfire IXs at Hornchurch in mid-1943. Otto Smik is kneeling second from left, and to his left, seated on the swinging chair, is Hornchurch Wing Leader, Tasmanian Wg Cdr John Ratten. At the other end of the chair is Smik's CO, Sqn Ldr E J F Harrington, whilst the Slovakian pilot's dog can be seen sitting in front of the Australian pilot at the extreme right of the photo! (via Jiri Rajlich)

LEFT Flg Off Smik poses with a Spitfire IX at Hornchurch in the late summer of 1943. The Slovakian ace flew a variety of No 222 Sqn aircraft during his scoring spree, which saw him claim four Fw 190s and two and one shared Bf 109s between 15 July and 27 September (via Zdenek Hurt)

'The new 1600 hp Merlin 61 engine that powered the Spitfire Mk IX was designed for use in heavy bombers, but it was soon found that it could be housed in an extended Spitfire Mk V airframe. Individual ejector exhausts were fitted, and a four-blade Rotol airscrew absorbed the extra engine power at high altitudes. The supercharger cut in automatically at about 19,000 ft (6000 m), which gave a top speed of about 410 mph (660 kmh). In short, the Spitfire Mk IX was the best fighting aeroplane of its day. Its great tactical advantage was that, apart from its longer nose and more numerous exhaust stacks, it looked exactly like the inferior Spitfire Mk V, and in the air the Germans would not know the difference – until we hit them.'

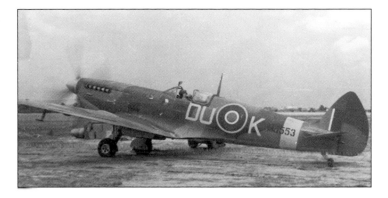

A typical No 312 Sqn Spitfire LF IXC is run up prior to being taxied out onto the Sommerfeld track at Appledram in May 1944. This aircraft (MJ553) was converted into an LF IX the following month and issued to No 400 'City of Toronto' Sqn at RAF Odiham. It was in turn passed on to fellow RCAF unit No 414 'Sarnia Imperials' Sqn later that year and eventually lost to flak near Roermond on 7 November 1944 (*via Zdenek Hurt*)

PILOT BIOGRAPHY – OTTO SMIK

Born in January 1922 in Borzhom, near Tbilisi in the Soviet Union (now Georgia), Otto Smik lived in the Slovakian part of Czechoslovakia until the German occupation in 1938. Fleeing across western Europe, he eventually arrived in England and joined the RAF. Following the completion of his training in 1942, Smik was posted to No 131 Sqn at RAF Westhampnett, on the Sussex coast. His flight commander was future Spitfire ace Flt Lt R W F 'Sammy' Sampson, who remembers;

'Smik I knew to be a very affable chap, who spoke German, some Dutch, French, his native Czech of course, and pretty good English.'

Smik joined No 122 Sqn at RAF Hornchurch, in Essex, in 1943, claiming a probable kill with the unit on 13 March. He moved yet again in the early summer, this time to No 222 Sqn, although as the latter unit was a part of the Hornchurch Wing at the time, he simply swapped dispersals. Smik really found his mark with No 222 Sqn, scoring 6.5 kills in three months – successes that resulted in him receiving the DFC.

He joined forces with his fellow countrymen in early 1944 when he was posted to No 310 'Czech' Sqn at Appledram, east of Portsmouth. A further 2.5 kills followed with the unit in June 1944, as well as three V1s in a single sortie on 8 July.

Smik then became a flight commander with No 312 'Czech' Sqn at RAF North Weald, in Essex, before being posted in November to No 127 Sqn at Grimbergen, in Belgium, as the unit's new CO. He lasted just two weeks in the job, however, for he was killed when his Spitfire IX (RR229) was downed by flak during an attack on a heavily defended rail goods yard in the Arnhem area on the 28th of the month. His wingman was also lost during this action.

SPECIFICATION

Supermarine Spitfire HF IXC

TYPE:	single-engined monoplane fighter
ACCOMMODATION:	pilot
DIMENSIONS:	length 31 ft 1 in (9.47 m) wingspan 36 ft 10 in (11.23 m) height 12 ft 7.75 in (3.86 m)
WEIGHTS:	empty 5816 (kg) maximum take-off 9500 lb (4309 kg)
PERFORMANCE:	maximum speed 416 mph (kmh) range 980 miles (1577 km) with external tanks powerplant Rolls-Royce Merlin 70 output 1475 hp (kW)
ARMAMENT:	HF IXC, two 20 mm cannon and four 0.303 in machine guns in wings; provision for 1000-lb (454-kg) bombload externally
FIRST FLIGHT DATE:	27 September 1941
OPERATORS:	Australia, Canada, New Zealand, South Africa, UK, USA, USSR
PRODUCTION:	5665

Through the desperate years of 1941-42, the Spitfire was outclassed by firstly the Bf 109F/G and then the potent Fw 190. Indeed, it was the appearance of the 'Butcher bird' from Focke-Wulf on the Channel Front in September 1941 which provided the impetus for a new version of Spitfire to help restore the balance – thus was born the Spitfire Mk IX. Built as a stop-gap fighter until the comprehensively re-engineered Mks VII and VIII could be put into production, the IX comprised a lightly-modified Mk V airframe fitted with an uprated Merlin 61 engine. Despite its temporary nature, the 'new' fighter was so warmly received by frontline units within Fighter Command that no less than 5665 were built between 1942-45. The secret to the 'new' Spitfire's success can be directly attributed to its Rolls-Royce powerplant, which had been fitted with a two-stage/two-speed supercharger that would cut in automatically at pre-determined altitudes, but could also be manually controlled at lower ceilings. The earlier Mk V, powered by the Merlin 45, had had to make do with a single-stage/single-speed supercharger, which was fine at low to medium altitude, but rather 'breathless' at more rarefied ceilings above 20,000 ft – the chosen battleground of the *Jagdwaffe*. The Merlin 61 changed all this, however, as its more powerful supercharger forced a greater volume of air through the engine cylinders, and thus prevented performance tailing off in the thinner altitudes that Fighter Command was having to fight in.

Spitfire HF IXC ML296/'DU-N' of Flt Lt Otto Smik, No 312 Sqn, North Weald, September 1944

This aircraft was Otto Smik's personal mount for much of his time as 'B Flight' Commander with No 312 Sqn. It carries his full tally of nine aircraft and three V1s destroyed, plus a Czechoslovakian air force roundel and a No 312 Sqn emblem. ML296 was originally delivered new to No 74 Sqn at North Weald on 4 May 1944, and was then passed to No 312 Sqn on 8 July. The fighter was allocated to Smik when he arrived on the unit soon afterwards, and he was shot down by flak in it whilst strafing Gilze-Rijen

airfield, in Holland, on 3 September – No 312 Sqn had been tasked with escorting Halifaxes sent to bomb nearby Soesterberg on this day. Smik crash-landed ML296 near Breda, in Holland, and was helped by a Dutch family to reach Allied lines. He finally returned to No 312 Sqn on 29 October.

McCampbell
and
Minsi III

'Indubitably, the most exciting action I ever had in combat occurred during the battles of Leyte Gulf.'

Ranking US Navy ace of all time, and premier Hellcat exponent, Cdr David McCampbell waged his own personal war on a large formation of Japanese aircraft on the morning of 24 October 1944 – the opening day of the Battle of Leyte Gulf. Already the Navy's leading ace going into this action, CAG McCampbell had been warned by his superiors that his loss in combat would be a serious blow to morale, and at 34 years of age, he should let the younger charges in VF-15 take the fight to the Japanese. However, on this day all of USS *Essex's* fighter pilots were needed to defend the task force, and McCampbell insisted that he was still a 'fighter pilot', so should launch too.

Owing to the fact that the commander was not scheduled to fly, and that his F6F-5 Hellcat (BuNo 70143), *Minsi III*, was never flown by anyone else, the fighter had been spotted in the hangar deck unprimed for combat. When word was received that the CAG was to launch, it was hurriedly brought up to the 'roof' and filled with as much fuel as time permitted – a full drop tank and partially full fuselage tanks. In this configuration, he launched from *Essex* in near record time, leading the last seven Hellcats of 'Fighting 15' skyward to intercept an incoming raid of awesome proportions. Lighting a cigarette, the CAG assessed the situation

Cdr David McCampbell's nine-kill exploits of 24 October 1944 saw his tally jump to 30 victories, and his successes during the Battle of Leyte Gulf partially offset the news for the 'folks back home' of the loss of the light carrier USS *Princeton* in action that same morning. F6F-5 *Minsi III* (BuNo 70143) was quickly polished up and decorated with 30 victory flags, and its pilot photographed in various poses for the national papers (*Tailhook*)

Iain Wyllie

and went to work. His account of the following action was typically understated;

'Indubitably, the most exciting action I ever had in combat occurred during the battles of Leyte Gulf. On my first flight on the morning of 24 October 1944, I was launched from the USS *Essex* with a group of Grumman Hellcats to intercept an incoming raid of a hundred-odd Japs. This was the second and last time I was to take part in a "fighter scramble", primarily because my job as Air Group Commander did not normally demand that I engage in this type of combat. Also, after the action, our Admiral said to me, "It's alright this time, but don't let it happen again".

'We intercepted the raids about 20 miles from the task group. This incident met the highest expectations of my fondest hopes and dreams of favourable combat conditions. Due to my experience in the previous four months of combat, plus the luck of the Irish, I was able to exploit the situation. Without attempting to explain the action in detail, suffice it to say that I did what came naturally to one who had spent many years training for just such an occasion.

'My wingman and I accounted for 15 definitely destroyed. I was credited with nine shot down and two probables. Not a single enemy plane got through to attack our ships. After following the decimated formation nearly all the way to Manila, we returned to the vicinity of the task group, exhausted of ammunition and near fuel-exhaustion, to witness the agonised manoeuvres of our ships under attack by a second raid – which caused mortal damage to USS *Princeton*. I landed aboard the *Langley* since it had the only clear deck in the task group that could take me, and barely had enough gas to taxy out of the arresting gear.

'When the final tally was in, the seven planes I had led were credited with 27 enemy aircraft destroyed and an additional eight planes probably destroyed. We only had superficial damage, largely as a result of flying through the debris of exploding enemy planes.'

ABOVE This photograph, taken on the morning of 21 October 1944, shows CAG-15 David McCampbell taxying forward to his shutdown spot on *Essex* after completing a sweep over Tablas Island, in the Philippines. He had downed a 'Dinah' and a 'Nate' during this sortie, thus assuming the mantle of the US Navy's ranking carrier ace from Alex Vraciu of VF-16 (*via Jim Sullivan*)

BELOW Just days after the successful conclusion to the first Battle of the Philippine Sea in June 1944, Cdr McCampbell replaced his late-build F6F-3, nicknamed *The Minsi*, with this factory-fresh F6F-5. Looking resplendent in its Glossy Sea Blue scheme, the CAG's *Minsi II* has its engine and fuel system cleared of inhibitor off Saipan prior to being deemed fit for ops. One of the first F6F-5s issued to Air Group 15, this aircraft was flown infrequently in comparison with McCampbell's previous Hellcats, as its pilot was not fond of its engine unreliability. Indeed, the fighter suffered two powerplant failures in very short order whilst the CAG was at the controls, and following air combat damage, it was renamed and passed on to a line pilot from VF-15 (*Tailhook*)

PILOT BIOGRAPHY – DAVID McCAMPBELL

Born in Bessemer, Alabama, in January 1910, David McCampbell entered the Naval Academy at Annapolis in 1929 and graduated into the naval reserve as an ensign in June 1933. Called to active duty the following year, he served on the cruiser USS *Portland* from June 1934 through to June 1937, spending time as an observer flying in the ship's Curtiss SOC floatplane during the final 18 months of his posting.

Upon leaving the *Portland*, McCampbell entered flight training and was designated a Naval Aviator in April 1938. He was duly posted to VF-4 and flew Grumman F3F-1s biplane fighters from the deck of the USS *Ranger* until May 1940, when he joined *Wasp's* Air Group as a Landing Signals Officer. McCampbell was still serving with this carrier when it was sunk off Guadalcanal by a Japanese submarine in September 1942. A shore tour followed, before he helped to form VF-15 in September 1943 and embarked with the unit as its CO aboard the USS *Essex*. Promoted to Commander Air Group 15 in February 1944, McCampbell was to enjoy unrivalled success during his time as boss of this air group.

His first kills came during the Battle of the Philippine Sea in mid June, and by the time this action had finished, McCampbell had scored 10.5 victories in 12 days – including an incredible seven and one probable on the 19th. He went two better during the Battle of Leyte Gulf in October, and by the time his scoring run came to an end on 14 November, Cdr McCampbell's tally had reached 34 destroyed, 5 probables and 1 damaged.

Awarded the Congressional Medal of Honor for his outstanding exploits, McCampbell remained in the navy postwar, attaining captain rank and commanding the carrier USS *Bon Homme Richard* in 1959-60. He retired in July 1964 and passed away in West Palm Beach, Florida, on 30 June 1996

SPECIFICATION

Grumman F6F-3 Hellcat

TYPE:	single-engined monoplane fighter
ACCOMMODATION:	pilot
DIMENSIONS:	length 33 ft 4 in (10.16 m) wingspan 42 ft 10 in (13.06 m) height 14 ft 5 in (4.40 m)
WEIGHTS:	empty 9042 lb (4101 kg) maximum take-off 13,228 lb (6000 kg)
PERFORMANCE:	maximum speed 376 mph (605 kmh) range 1085 miles (1746 km) powerplant Pratt & Whitney R-2800-10W Double Wasp output 2000 hp (1491 kW)
ARMAMENT:	six 0.50 in machine guns in wings; provision for six rockets under wings or 2000 lb (907 kg) of bombs under centre section
FIRST FLIGHT DATE:	26 June 1942
OPERATORS:	UK, USA
PRODUCTION:	4403

The F6F embodied the early lessons learnt by users of Grumman's previous fleet fighter, the F4F Wildcat, in the Pacific, as well as general pointers from the air war in Europe. Following receipt of the US Navy's order for the fighter in June 1941, Grumman modified the 'paper' aircraft by lowering the wing centre section to enable the undercarriage to be wider splayed, fitted more armour-plating around the cockpit to protect the pilot and increased the size of the fighter's ammunition magazines. Less than a year after being ordered, the prototype XF6F-1 made its first flight, and it was soon realised that a more powerful engine was needed to give the fighter a combat edge – the Pratt & Whitney R-2800-10 was duly installed, resulting in the F-1 being redesignated an F-3. The aircraft made its operational debut in August 1943, and from that point on, the question of aerial supremacy in the Pacific was never in doubt. Pilots flying the Hellcat would claim over 5200 kills in the Pacific between 1943-45, and more than 300 naval aviators achieved ace status in the Grumman fighter. Amazingly, only three major variants were produced – the -3, the improved -5 and the -3N/-5N nightfighters. The Fleet Air Arm was also a great believer in the Hellcat, procuring almost 1200 between 1943-45.

VF-15 pipped VF-18 to the title of 'Topguns' for the Leyte action by a mere 1.5 kills – 140.5 versus 139! This group shot of 'Fighting Fifteen' was taken just days before it was replaced on *Essex* by VF-4 on 17 November. VF-15 produced 26 aces during its seven months at sea, and the backdrop for this end of deployment photo is provided by Cdr McCampbell's *Minsi III*. Its pilot is seated to the immediate right of the squadron emblem that adorns its scoreboard (*via the National Museum of Naval Aviation*)

F6F-5 BuNo 70143/*Minsi III* of Cdr David McCampbell, Commander Air Group 15, USS *Essex*, 25 October 1944

Easily the best-known Hellcat of them all, BuNo 70143 was an early production F6F-5 that retained the 'windows' behind the cockpit as per the F6F-3 – a feature deleted on most 'Dash Fives'. As an air group commander, McCampbell was able to fly his assigned aircraft on nearly every mission, and this particular Hellcat lasted far longer than either of his previous *Minsis*. Although McCampbell lost his logbooks after the war, it is estimated that he scored 20 or more of his 34 confirmed victories in *Minsi III*. This machine was duly lost in an accident in December 1944 whilst being flown by McCampbell's replacement.

OLD CROW OVER GERMANY

'I clobber a Focke-Wulf right off, but he rolls into a dive too quickly for me to tell if he's had it.'

Well into his second tour with the 357th FG, and just a day away from being promoted to major a full six weeks shy of his 23rd birthday, Clarence E 'Bud' Anderson scored his final kills during a bomber escort mission to Berlin on 5 December 1944. Two Fw 190s destroyed and a third as a probable took his tally to 16.25, ranking him third in the group's long list of aces. Anderson recounted this mission in his excellent autobiography, *To Fly and Fight;*

   "'As we approached the target", says the combat report I filed on December 5, "we went north and intercepted about 20 Fw 190s". Well, what it didn't say was that one of my flight members got the bends on the way in to the target at 31,000 ft, so we had to descend to where he was comfortable again. Since I couldn't very well let him go down alone, I took the whole flight down. And since there was no point in just flying in circles, we made a sweep to the north of the bomber stream. Sure enough, we ran into some Fw 190s forming up and bounced them hard.

   'I clobber a Focke-Wulf right off, but he rolls into a dive too quickly for me to tell if he's had it. There are '190s all over the place, so I write it off as a probable. Later, my wingman, in his debriefing, will emphatically call this a kill.

   'I go after another. I've been at high altitude a long time, my airplane is cold – and as we dive into warmer air my canopy suddenly goes snow white with frost! This will get your attention.

This official AAF photograph of a youthful Capt Clarence E 'Bud' Anderson was taken at Leiston during the spring of 1944 (*via 'Bud' Anderson*)

If there is one thing in combat that will frighten the hell out of a pilot, it's suddenly going blind. Cursing the lousy defroster, I throw the plane over and make a quick exit, frantically wiping the glass with my glove.

'My pawing clears the windscreen in a couple of seconds, and here I am, sitting pretty, right in back of four Focke-Wulfs sliding in and out of a layer of haze. I close on the last one in line and open fire up close. My tracers claw at the canopy, blow it away. The stricken '190 lurches and falls, disappearing into the undercast, the cockpit ablaze. I turn my attention to the number three man, give him a burst at long range, and see flashes all over the cockpit area. He goes spinning down, too, trailing smoke.

'I pull up, again looking for targets, and a Messerschmitt is suddenly right there in front of me, his landing gear down. There is no sound reason why a pilot would be flying around with his landing gear down. But reasons don't matter to me. Tough luck either way, pal. He makes a climbing turn to the right, and my sights are just full of him. There is no way to miss him. I trigger the guns, and they quit almost instantly. They had spit maybe ten rounds. Now the silence is deafening. Damn!

'After landing at Leiston, claiming two for sure and one probable, I found that I'd expended 680 rounds. I brought home 1200 – two-thirds of the ammo I'd left with. I took it in my stride. Gun trouble was hardly uncommon with the P-51.'

During the course of his two tours with the 357th FG, 'Bud' Anderson was assigned four Mustangs – three P-51Bs and a solitary P-51D. The latter aircraft was used exclusively during his second tour, which ran from September 1944 through to January 1945. In that time, the Mustang (44-14450) went from this overall olive drab (OD) scheme to natural metal (*via 'Bud' Anderson*)

OLD CROW, now stripped of its OD paint, sits in a snow-covered revetment at Leiston just days after 'Bud' Anderson had scored his final kills. The OD scheme was a favourite of the 357th FG, who retained it long after other groups had reverted to flying natural metal Mustangs, Thunderbolts and Lightnings – at least the 110-gallon 'paper' drop tank still wears matt grey paint! The 357th was also one of the last to remove the 'D-Day stripes' from its P-51s (*via 'Bud' Anderson*)

Taken on the same day as the wintry Leiston photograph (note the snow on the pilot's boot), now Maj 'Bud' Anderson sits on the wing of his faithful P-51D-10 *OLD CROW*. 'I tell my non-drinking friends that all my fighters were named after the smartest bird that flies in the sky, the crow, but my drinking buddies all know they were named after that good old Kentucky straight bourbon whiskey!', remarked the triple ace in his foreword for this volume (*via 'Bud' Anderson*)

PILOT BIOGRAPHY – 'BUD' ANDERSON

A native of Oakland, California, Clarence E 'Bud' Anderson entered the Army Air Corps' Aviation Cadet Program in January 1942, being rated a pilot some nine months later at Luke Field, Arizona. Initially assigned to the P-39-equipped 328th FG, 2Lt Anderson flew defensive patrols along the Pacific coast from Oakland Municipal Airport, in the San Francisco Bay area.

Some months later he became a founder member of the 363rd FS, which was part of the equally new 357th FG that had been activated at Tonopah, in the Nevada desert, on 1 December 1942. As with the 328th FG, this new group was also assigned Airacobras. Anderson was sent overseas with the 357th in late November 1943, sailing to Britain on the *Queen Elizabeth* – 'the biggest target in the history of warfare, unless you count cities', was how he described the majestic 83,000-ton ocean liner!

The 357th FG was destined to become the first fighter group in the Eighth Air Force to be equipped with the Merlin-engined Mustang, commencing operations from Leiston, in Suffolk, in February 1944. 'Bud' Anderson soon proved his ability in combat, and by the time his first combat tour came to an end in July, his score stood at 12.25 victories. Following a spell on leave in the USA, he returned to complete a second tour, raising his final tally to 16.25 kills. Anderson had flown 116 missions in less than a year, and had never been hit by enemy fire or aborted a sortie.

Remaining in the air force postwar, he spent time as a test pilot, commanded the Sabre-equipped 69th FBS in Korea in the mid-1950s and saw action over Vietnam in the F-105 Thunderchief whilst in command of the 355th TFW in 1970. Col Anderson retired from the USAF in 1972 to join McDonnell Aircraft Company, and he subsequently served for 12 years with the aerospace giant at Edwards AFB as manager of its flight test facility. Despite having recently turned 78, 'Bud' Anderson still flies a privately-owned P-51D Mustang at various airshows across North America.

P-51D-10 Mustang 44-14450/*OLD CROW* of Capt Clarence E 'Bud' Anderson, 363rd FS/357th FG, Leiston, November 1944

Despite the P-51D being present at Leiston from May 1944 onwards, 'Bud' Anderson had flown a B-model Mustang throughout his first tour. He explained why in his autobiography; 'The Ds had begun arriving in the spring of 1944, and I got my own when I came back from leave. I could have had one of the first ones in May, but my earlier B-model was working so well, and I was so close to the end of my tour, that rather than take some new airplane and shake all the bugs out, I decided to stay with the *OLD CROW* I had'. This aircraft had originally boasted OD camouflage, but in November it was stripped off by his dedicated groundcrew. 'Bud' Anderson again; 'Stripping the paint off a Mustang was no simple thing. It is no simple thing to take the paint off a car, and a P-51 is much bigger. Stripping OLD CROW figured to take several men several days, but there was no urgency to do it – the next time I took some time off would be fine – and so I put my name down on the board for the next morning's mission. When I walked to my aircraft the following morning, it was gleaming bare metal. My groundcrew – Otto Heino, Mel Schueneman and Leo Zimmermann – had stayed up the whole night through, hand-rubbing the paint off with rags soaked in gasoline. In the process, they had rubbed most of the skin off their hands too'. Anderson claimed four Fw 190s destroyed and two as probables flying 44-14450.

SPECIFICATION

North American P-51D/K Mustang

TYPE:	single-engined monoplane fighter
ACCOMMODATION:	pilot
DIMENSIONS:	length 32 ft 3 in (9.83 m)
	wingspan 37 ft 0 in (11.28 m)
	height 12 ft 2 in (3.71 m)
WEIGHTS:	empty 7635 lb (3463 kg)
	maximum take-off 12,100 lb (5488 kg)
PERFORMANCE:	maximum speed 437 mph (703 kmh)
	range 1650 miles (2655 km) with external tanks
	powerplant Packard V-1650-7
	output 1720 hp (1283 kW)
ARMAMENT:	six 0.50 in machine guns in wings; up to 2000 lb (907 kg) of bombs or six 5 in (12.7 cm) rocket projectiles under wings
FIRST FLIGHT DATE:	17 November 1943
OPERATORS:	Australia, China, the Netherlands, New Zealand, South Africa, UK, USA
PRODUCTION:	9493

The P-51D was effectively an improved version of the B/C-model that had first been fitted with the Merlin 61 engine in late 1942. One of the major complaints from Eighth Air Force fighter pilots who debuted the revised Mustang in combat in early 1944 centred on the poor rearward visibility on offer. North American quickly set about rectifying this with the follow-on P-51D, which was designed from the outset to feature a cut-down rear fuselage and a 360-degree clear vision tear-drop canopy. The new variant also boasted an additional two 0.50 in machine guns in the wings, although the engine remained the same as was installed in late-production P-51B/Cs – the licence-produced Packard V-1650-7. The first D-model Mustangs arrived in the ETO just prior to D-Day, and the aircraft had replaced all 'razorback' P-51s in-theatre by year-end. Despite its better visibility and improved armament, the newer model was not universally welcomed by all, as Lt Elmer O'Dell of the 363rd FG explained; 'I flew all of my missions in the same P-51B-10, and in June 1944 I was offered a P-51D, but I preferred to keep the B-10. I checked out the D and flew a number of mock combat missions in it, but to me it didn't have the delicate response of the B-10, which had four 0.50-calibre guns. When they built the D they added another gun to each wing. To do so, they had to alter the configuration of the wing. I maintain this caused a small reduction in manoeuvrability. I guess it was a personal thing, for obviously most pilots thought otherwise'.

ACE IN A DAY

'The plane immediately began to burn, spinning off to the left.'

When Col Dave Schilling became an 'ace in a day' on 23 December 1944, he was already a combat veteran with 18.5 kills to his name. Boss of the 56th FG, on this day he was leading 56 P-47s of 'Zemke's Wolfpack' in support of a maximum effort raid by VIII Bomber Command, which had been hastily organised in response to Hitler's Ardennes offensive. The mission took the fighters across Holland and into Germany where, at 1145, the Thunderbolts clashed with at least 90 Fw 190s and Bf 109s from JGs 4, 11, 27 and 54 (*via Ian Phillips*)

'I flew straight ahead, pulled up, applied full power, and made a slow diving turn to the left to position my flight on the outside and allow the other three to cross over inside so that we might bring as many planes into position to fire as possible. In so doing, I managed to hit the rear right Me 109 with about a 20-degree deflection shot at a range of about 700 yards. There was a large concentration of strikes all over the left side of the fuselage, and he fell off to the left.

'I then picked out another fighter more or less ahead of the first and fired from about the same range as the first, causing him to smoke and catch fire immediately. By this time the first Me 109 was slightly ahead, below and to the left, at which point he started to smoke and caught fire. I then picked another and fired at about 1000 yards and missed as he broke right and started to dive for the deck. At about 17,000 ft I had closed to about 500 yards and fired, resulting in a heavy concentration of strikes, and the pilot bailed out.

'At this point I had become separated from the other three flights and had only my own with me. I heard Maj Comstock of the 63rd FS in a hell of a fight, and called to get his position. As I was attempting to locate him, I sighted another gaggle of 35-40 Fw 190s 1000 ft below, circling to the left. I repeated the same tactics as before and attacked one from 500 yards' range and slightly above and to the left. The plane immediately began to burn, spinning off to the left. I then fired at a second and got two or three strikes. He immediately took violent evasive action, and it took me several minutes of manoeuvring until I managed to get into a position to fire. I fired from about 300 yards above and to the left, and he forced me to pull through him and fire as he went out of sight over the cowling. I gave him a five-second burst and

Iain Wyllie

RIGHT Mechanics work on the engine of Maj Dave Schilling's assigned P-47D-1 42-7938/'LM-S' on 3 September 1943 after 'Hub' Zemke had collected a little battle damage whilst using it to lead two missions on this day. When an assigned aircraft was out of service for repair, maintenance or modification, the pilot, if scheduled to fly, was allocated another squadron aircraft. Group HQ officers usually took the assigned fighter of another HQ officer. Schilling's P-47D-1 was a War Bond subscription aircraft named *Hewlett-Woodmere Long Island*, and he used it to down 3.5 aircraft (all Fw 190s) and damage an Me 210/410 during October-November 1943. In the background of this photograph, 'Pappy' Craig's 'LM-R' can be seen near the farmhouse dubbed 'Schilling's Acres', which was used by the 62nd FS (*via Roger Freeman*)

BELOW This 'Wolfpack' ace quartet are made up of (from left to right) 'Hub' Zemke, Dave Schilling, 'Gabby' Gabreski and Fred Christensen, all of whom are setting an example to their fellow officers by wearing standard issue uniforms. Between them, the four aces downed 90 German aircraft during World War 2 (*via Jerry Scutts*)

began getting strikes all over him. The pilot immediately bailed out and the ship spun down to the left, smoking and burning, until it blew up at about 15,000 ft.

'By this time I was alone, and saw a 63rd FS plane. I called, and he joined up just as a 35–40 plane formation of Fw 190s flew by heading west about 1000 ft above. I had hoped to sneak by and turn upon their tails, but they saw me just as I started my climbing turn. I knew I would have to hit the deck sooner or later, but I thought I could get their tail-end man before I had to. My wingman lagged back, and just as I was getting set, he called and said two were on his tail. I though I saw him get hit and told him to do vertical aileron rolls and hit the deck. At that time two got behind me and were getting set, so I did several rolls as I started down, hit the switch and outran them by a mile as I got to the deck. I lost them and zoomed back up to 8000 ft.'

Dave Schilling claimed five kills in this P-47D-25 (42-26641) on 23 December 1944, and these proved to be his only successes with the aircraft. This action was the 56th FG's last big dogfight of the war, and pilots from the group emerged with 34 victories (*via Roger Freeman*)

SPECIFICATION

Republic P-47D Thunderbolt

TYPE:	single-engined monoplane fighter
ACCOMMODATION:	pilot
DIMENSIONS:	length 36 ft 1.75 in (11.02 m)
	wingspan 40 ft 9.75 in (12.44 m)
	height 14 ft 1.75 in (4.31 m)
WEIGHTS	empty 10,000 lb (4536 kg)
	maximum take-off 17,500 lb (7938 kg)
PERFORMANCE:	maximum speed 426 mph (686 kmh)
	range 1800 miles (2897 km) with external tanks
	powerplant Pratt & Whitney R-2800-59W
	Double Wasp
	output 2535 hp (1890.3 kW)
ARMAMENT:	eight 0.50 in machine guns in wings; two 1000-lb
	(454-kg) or three 500-lb (227-kg) bombs or ten 5 in
	(12.7 mm) rockets externally
FIRST FLIGHT DATE:	6 May 1941 (XP-47B)
OPERATORS:	Brazil, France, Mexico, UK, USA, USSR
PRODUCTION:	12,065

PILOT BIOGRAPHY – DAVE SCHILLING

Born on 15 December 1918 in the army town of Leavenworth, Kansas, Dave Schilling would go on to attend prestigious Dartmouth College, graduating in 1939. Soon after he joined the army, enlisting as a flying cadet, and then went on to become commissioned as a second lieutenant on 11 May 1940 at Brooks Field in Texas. Originally assigned to the newly-formed 56th FG in June 1941, he then joined the P-40E-equipped 63rd FS.

With the start of the war Schilling was soon promoted, making captain by 1 March 1942 and subsequently assuming command of the 62nd FS. In June of that year the 56th FG received P-47Bs in advance of its move to Britain. It arrived in the ETO in December-January, and Schilling flew his first combat mission during April 1943. He achieved ace status in early October, and by mid-August 1944 had become the 56th FG's commanding officer. Promoted to full colonel, Schilling held this position until 27 January 1945. By the end of the war, he had flown 132 combat missions and claimed 22.5 kills.

A career officer, Schilling stayed in the postwar air force and assumed, once again, command of the 56th FG on 24 April 1946. By this time, the group was based at Selfridge Field, in Michigan, and converting to the new P-80 Shooting Star. On 7 July 1948, he led the 56th on an epic flight to Fürstenfeldbruck airfield, in Berlin, returning two weeks later to establish the feasibility of jet fighter ferry flights across the Atlantic. Schilling would continue pioneering jet flights, as well as advancing in rank, until his untimely death on 14 August 1956 in a car accident in Suffolk, England.

P-47Bs joined the Eighth Air Force in Britain in late 1942, with aircraft being issued to the 4th and 56th FGs. Built to absorb much damage, and rock steady as a gun platform, the Thunderbolt was given the crucial bomber escort mission for the B-17 and B-24 groups that were carrying out hazardous daylight raids on targets located deep within 'Fortress Europe'. Initial encounters with German fighters were not encouraging, for the P-47 was easily outmanoeuvred at low to medium altitudes, and its engine performance was deemed to be lacklustre. The Republic fighter was also struggling to stay with the bombers for the duration of their missions because of inadequate internal fuel tankage. However, the arrival of the first drop tank-equipped P-47Cs in mid-1943 addressed the endurance problem, and the implementation of better combat tactics tailored around the strong points of the Thunderbolt resulted in VIII Fighter Command (FC) boasting a handful of aces by the autumn of 1943. The arrival of the definitive P-47D in late 1943 was followed shortly after by the 'bubble top' Thunderbolt, which soon became the favoured mount of most fighter pilots thanks to its superior rearward visibility. Nine fighter groups made use of the P-47 within the Eighth Air Force, although only one – the 56th FG – was still equipped with the Thunderbolt by VE-Day, the rest having transitioned to P-51D/Ks. No fewer than 64 VIII FC pilots 'made ace' on the P-47 in this theatre, and the 56th FG finished the war as the Eighth's highest-scoring fighter group, claiming 677 aerial kills.

P-47D-25 42-26641 of Col Dave Schilling, CO of the 56th FG, Boxted, December 1944
One of seven P-47s assigned to Dave Schilling during his time with the 56th FG, this fighter revealed an early 'Wolfpack' penchant for painting *Dogpatch* cartoon characters on its Thunderbolts by featuring a neat rendering of 'Hairless Joe' on its cowling – although the name of the Al Capp character was not applied. Schilling's penultimate aircraft (he was subsequently issued with P-47M-1 44-21125/'HV-S', but engine problems saw it grounded), this D-25 was used by the colonel for his 'five in a day' haul on 23 December 1944, raising his final tally to 22.5-0-6.

THE FLYING UNDERTAKER

'As I closed on the fighter's tail, he levelled out. I closed to point-blank range and fired a burst that started black smoke streaming from his engine exhaust stacks.'

Proudly wearing his Congressional Medal of Honor around his neck, Maj William Shomo poses for the camera at Binmaley, on Luzon, on 3 April 1945. The medal was awarded to him on this day by Gen Ennis C Whitehead, Commander of the Fifth Air Force (*via John Stanaway*)

The Fifth Air Force produced just one Mustang ace during World War 2, but he did down seven of his eight kills in a solitary sortie! On the morning of 11 January 1945, Capt William Shomo, CO of the 71st Tactical Reconnaissance Group's 81st Tactical Reconnaissance Squadron (TRS), and his wingman, Lt Paul Lipscomb, set out on an armed recce to Atarri and Laoag airstrips on the Philippine island of Luzon. En route, they spotted a single G4M 'Betty' bomber, escorted by no fewer than 11 Ki-61s and a solitary Ki-44, through a break in thin cloud. Rushing in to engage the unsuspecting enemy, Shomo and Lipscomb hit the left formation of 'Tonys' first, downing four fighters in quick succession from close range. The former then manoeuvred his F-6D-10 (44-14841) in behind the second element on the right side, as his combat report details;

'The second element of two "Tonys" on the right side of the formation turned to the left and started after my wingman, who was moving down on the remaining element of two "Tonys" on the left side. As this element crossed over, they passed directly in front of me, and I fired a burst into the wingman and he exploded in flames. Lt Lipscomb then fired at the wingman of the first

Nicknamed *SNOOKS-5th*, this was the F-6D used by Capt William Shomo to shoot down six Ki-61 'Tony' fighters and a lone G4M 'Betty' bomber on 11 January 1945. Note the 250-lb bomb under the fighter's left wing and the camera port to the right of the fuselage star. The Mustang was photographed at Leyte in late January 1945 (*Krane files*)

This publicity photo shows Capt Shomo overseeing the painting of eight victory flags forward of the cockpit of *SNOOKS-5th* the day after his famous engagement. His first kill had been claimed 24 hours prior to his seven-victory haul (*via John Stanaway*)

element on the left side and this "Tony" also burst into flames. Lt Lipscomb then made a pass on the bomber, but apparently did no damage. I then started to make a pass on the bomber, and as I closed on its tail from the right quarter, a rear gunner started to fire at me, so I dropped my wing tanks to be less vulnerable. I

dropped below the bomber and raked the underside of the fuselage with a long burst. The right wing root caught fire and black smoke started streaming behind the bomber as I passed under and beyond it.

'I started up in a steep climb to the left, and at this point I saw my wingman's third victory as he hit a "Tony" in a head-on pass. It started to smoke and burn as it rolled into a vertical dive from about 600 ft. While still in the climbing turn, a "Tojo" started to fire at me from below, and with about 60° deflection. I tightened my climbing turn, and he skidded behind me, broke off and disappeared into the low hanging cloud.

'By this time I was headed in the original direction of the running fight, and saw the bomber crash in the field and burst into flames. I also saw two "Tonys" in element formation, just beyond where the bomber crashed, flying south at an altitude of approximately 800 ft. I pursued them, closed on the lead "Tony", and fired a burst into him from the rear. This "Tony" exploded and broke up in mid-air. The other "Tony" broke to the right, and dove steeply to an altitude of approximately 300 ft, and as I closed on the fighter's tail, he levelled out. I closed to point-blank range and fired a burst that started black smoke streaming from his engine exhaust stacks. I was overrunning this "Tony", so I swerved out to the right side and above him. The "Tony" went into a gentle dive toward the ground. I snapped a picture with the oblique camera mounted on the fuselage of my airplane just before the "Tony" struck the ground and burst into flames.'

PILOT BIOGRAPHY – WILLIAM SHOMO

Hailing from Jeanette, Pennsylvania, William Shomo's initial career choice saw him graduate from the Cincinnati College of Mortuary Research to the Pittsburgh School of Embalming! Having gained his qualifications and briefly practised as a licensed mortician, he then decided to join the army, serving as an aviation cadet from August 1941 through to March 1942. Shomo was posted to the South-west Pacific theatre in November 1943 as part of the 71st Reconnaissance Group (RG).

Based initially at Port Moresby, in New Guinea, he flew both P-39Qs and P-40Ns on numerous photo-recce missions over enemy territory. In late 1944 his unit, the 82nd Tactical Reconnaissance Squadron (TRS), received a mix of 'straight' and camera-equipped (F-6D) Mustangs, which proved far more suited to the photo-recce mission. The 71st moved to the Philippines at around this time too, and following his promotion to captain, Shomo was given command of the 82nd TRS on Christmas Eve. Claiming his first kill on 10 January 1945, he went six better the following day, downing a bomber and six fighters over northern Luzon. Following this stunning action, he became only the second P-51 pilot of World War 2 to be awarded the Congressional Medal of Honor.

William Shomo remained in the air force postwar, seeing more action in the Korean War. Finally retiring from the USAF with the rank of lieutenant-colonel in September 1968, he passed away in his home state of Pennsylvania in June 1990, aged 72.

SPECIFICATION

North American P-51D/K Mustang

TYPE:	single-engined monoplane fighter
ACCOMMODATION:	pilot
DIMENSIONS:	length 32 ft 3 in (9.83 m)
	wingspan 37 ft 0 in (11.28 m)
	height 12 ft 2 in (3.71 m)
WEIGHTS:	empty 7635 lb (3463 kg)
	maximum take-off 12,100 lb (5488 kg)
PERFORMANCE:	maximum speed 437 mph (703 kmh)
	range 1650 miles (2655 km) with external tanks
	powerplant Packard V-1650-7
	output 1720 hp (1283 kW)
ARMAMENT:	six 0.50 in machine guns in wings; up to 2000 lb (907 kg) of bombs or six 5 in (12.7 cm) rocket projectiles under wings
FIRST FLIGHT DATE:	17 November 1943
OPERATORS:	Australia, China, the Netherlands, New Zealand, South Africa, UK, USA
PRODUCTION:	9493

Although William Shomo almost certainly used F-6D-10 44-14841 to score all of his kills, most of the surviving photos of the Medal of Honor winner and his Mustang feature P-51D-20 44-72505. Allocated to Shomo soon after his epic sortie, this aircraft was given a first-class paint job in anticipation of press coverage of its pilot's feat. Well photographed during the ensuing months, the Mustang was kept in almost spotless condition throughout this time. The fighter's nickname, *The FLYING UNDERTAKER*, was adopted by Shomo following incessant pestering from war corespondents, who had quickly seized on his unusual peacetime employment. All five of his previous aircraft (two P-39Qs, two P-40Ns and F-6D 44-14841) had carried the name *SNOOKS* (*via John Stanaway*)

With its long range, the Merlin Mustang was ideally suited to the island-hopping campaign waged in the Pacific. However, the defeat of Germany took precedence over all other theatres, and the first Mustangs for the Fifth Air Force only arrived in late 1944. These took the form of photo-recce F-6Ds for the 82nd TRS/71st TRG, and Capt William Shomo soon proved the aircraft's worth by downing seven aircraft in a single sortie on 11 January 1945 – he was the sole Mustang ace of the Fifth Air Force. Three P-51D/K-equipped groups joined the Seventh Air Force in the Pacific in early 1945, these aircraft making their combat debut over the Philippines. The groups really came into their own following the capture of the three airfields on Iwo Jima in late February, the 15th, 21st and 506th FGs all flying long-range B-29 escort missions from the island base until mid-August. These sorties often lasted a staggering eight hours, and during the final months of the war four Mustang pilots from the Seventh Air Force achieved 'acedom'. In the CBI (China-Burma-India), a small number of P-51As (and A-36As) had been introduced into combat in late 1943, although the Mustang only really began to have an impact on this forgotten theatre from mid-1944 onwards. P-51B/Cs and Ds were operated by the 1st and 2nd Air Commando Groups and the 23rd, 51st and 311th FGs, with ten aces being produced despite these groups conducting primarily ground-attack missions for the final year of the war.

F-6D-10 44-14841/*SNOOKS-5th* of Capt William Shomo, CO of the 82nd TRS/ 71st TRG, Leyte, January 1945

Shomo used this F-6D to down seven aircraft in one mission on 11 January 1945. A remarkably plain looking Mustang, its yellow fin tip marking was added after the aircraft's legendary sortie to denote its assignment to the 82nd TRS. Although not stated in the unit's documentation, or in the pilot's log book, it would seem likely that he also used this aircraft to down his only other kill, claimed 24 hours earlier. *SNOOKS-5th* suffered damage from flying debris shed by some of Shomo's seven victims on 11 January, so the boss of the 82nd TRS was issued with a near-new P-51D-20 in its place.

'RED 13'

'With the Me 262, they came in so fast it was point-blank firing.'

Although overwhelmingly outnumbered in the air, and hunted incessantly when on the ground, the select group of *Jagdflieger* who got to fly Messerschmitt's Me 262 in combat during the final months of the war left a lasting impression on those Allied airmen they came up against. Men such as S/Sgt Bernard J Byrnes, a gunner in B-26 Marauders with the 432nd BS/17th BG;

'The B-26 was a fine plane to be in during combat. However, those Me 262s were one terrible fighter to have to deal with. They came in so fast that you hardly had any time to lead them before they were on you using those four heavy calibre cannon. A normal fighter's range of fire was about 300 yards, and from a medium bomber like the B-26, we could fire with some accuracy out to about 600 yards, so we had a little advantage. But with the Me 262, they came in so fast it was point-blank firing. If the Germans had put those jets in the air sooner, it would have been very bad for us.'

Although those on the receiving end of an Me 262 attack were in serious trouble, the German pilot closing on his target also faced numerous difficulties, as legendary ace Generalleutnant Adolf Galland, *Verbandsführer* of JV 44, stated during interrogation just a matter of weeks after VE-Day;

'Because of the high cruising speed of a jet formation, which generally speaking was about 750 kmh (446 mph), it was relatively difficult to tell the exact direction of the approaching bombers. The reason for that was that one was not carrying out an observation from a fixed point, but was dashing through the air at such a pace that it was difficult to establish the relationship between the progress of the target and one's own direction. It could be done, but it needed a hell of a lot of practice. For that reason, the graduation of curves that one had to fly when positioning for an attack made things fairly difficult.

'Owing to the very high speed of the Me 262, it was also difficult to score a sufficient number of hits in the time available – in other words, to shoot well. During the final 1000 metres of the

An official Luftwaffe portrait of the then Hauptmann Heinz Bär, taken when awarded the Swords to his Knight's Cross with Oak Leaves in February 1942 (*via John Weal*)

Iain Wyllie

ABOVE Me 262A-1a 'Red 13' (Wk-Nr 110559) was the mount of Oberstleutnant Heinz Bär, *Kommandeur* of III./EJG 2 at Lager-Lechfeld in March 1945. Although he first flew the Me 262 in September 1944, it was not until January 1945 that Bär was posted to Lager-Lechfeld to command this *Gruppe*. Whilst III./EJG 2 was primarily a training unit, the ace nevertheless managed to achieve nine victories during his time as its CO, before being transferred to JV 44 during April 1945 as a substitute for the wounded Adolf Galland, who retained effective non-flying control. Once here, Bär continued to score freely, gaining his 16th, and final, jet victory on 28 April 1945 (*via Eddie Creek*)

RIGHT Prior to flying the Me 262, Heinz Bär was already one of the Luftwaffe's highest scoring pilots, with over 200 kills to his credit by the autumn of 1944. Not only was he a highly proficient ace, he was also a fine fighter leader (*via Eddie Creek*)

approach, the Me 262 should have been moving at a speed of at least 850 kmh (528 mph), as otherwise we would have been "money for jam" for the escort fighters. Sometimes though it wasn't necessary to fly that fast, and that made everything considerably easier.'

One man who conquered these, and myriad other obstacles associated with the pioneering jet fighter operations of 1944/45 was III./EJG 2's *Gruppenkommandeur*, Oberstleutnant Heinz Bär. He had claimed 204 kills on piston-engined fighters prior to transitioning to the Me 262A-1a in late 1944, and he would use all of this experience to become the most successful day jet fighter ace of World War 2 with 16 kills. He is seen in this artwork despatching a 387th BG B-26B Marauder whilst flying Me 262A-1a 'Red 13'(Wk-Nr 110559) on 9 April 1945 – one of two he claimed during the sortie. Within days of this action taking place, Bär was posted away from his *Gruppe's* Lager-Lechfeld base to Munich-Riem, where he joined JV 44.

Oberstleutnant Heinz Bär is seen sitting on the wing of 'Red 13' between sorties at Lager-Lechfeld in early 1945, discussing the maintenance of his jet with one of his 'blackmen' (*via Eddie Creek*)

SPECIFICATION

Messerschmitt Me 262A-1a

TYPE:	twin-engined monoplane jet fighter
ACCOMMODATION:	single-seat fighter-bomber or two-seat nightfighter
DIMENSIONS:	length 34 ft 9.5 in (10.60 m)
	wingspan 41 ft 0.5 in (12.51 m)
	height 11 ft 6.75 in (3.83 m)
WEIGHTS:	empty 9742 lb (4420 kg)
	normal loaded 14,101 lb (6396 kg)
PERFORMANCE:	maximum speed 540 mph (870 kmh)
	range 652 miles (1050 km)
	powerplants two Junkers Jumo 004B-1/-2 or -3 turbojet engines
	output 3960 lb st (17.8 kN)
ARMAMENT:	A-1a, four 30 mm cannon in nose and provision for 24 underwing rockets
FIRST FLIGHT DATE:	18 July 1942 (first all jet-powered flight)
OPERATORS:	Germany
PRODUCTION:	1433

PILOT BIOGRAPHY – HEINZ BÄR

In stark contrast to a number of his contemporaries, Heinz 'Pritzl' Bär's rise through the ranks was a long roller-coaster of a journey which lasted throughout the war from the first day of hostilities until the last.

Bär was a feldwebel when he scored his first victory – a French Hawk H-75A – during the 'Phoney War'. He also flew in the Battles of France and Britain which followed, surviving the latter conflict with 17 kills to his credit. Accompanying JG 51 to Russia, the now-commissioned Leutnant Bär received the Knight's Cross for 27 victories on 2 July 1941, and was awarded the Oak Leaves six weeks later after more than doubling his total to 60.

Having increased his score to 96 kills, and added the Swords to his Oak Leaves, Heinz Bär left the Eastern Front in the spring of 1942 to take command of I./JG 77 in the Mediterranean. He was now a proven fighter leader. Fiercely supportive of those serving under him, Bär was often outspoken to the point of insubordination when it came to their welfare. This did not always endear him to his superiors.

Consequently, although he duly served as *Kommodore* of both JGs 1 and 3, he also spent intervening periods in more lowly positions. Towards the close of the war he converted to the Me 262 jet fighter, and the last 16 of his 220 kills – this total including 21 heavy bombers – were achieved at the controls of this revolutionary aircraft.

Heinz Bär was himself shot down no fewer than 18 times during the war. The survivor of four bail-outs and fourteen crash-landings, Bär was tragically killed in a light aircraft accident in 1957.

The world's very first operational jet fighter, the Me 262 was also the most advanced aircraft of its generation to actually see combat. Design work on the Messerschmitt commenced as early as 1938, and the first tailwheeled prototype, fitted with a nose-mounted Junkers Jumo 210 piston engine, completed its maiden flight on 4 April 1941. Unfortunately for Messerschmitt, work on the aircraft's revolutionary turbojet powerplants failed to keep pace with their development of the airframe, and it was not until 18 July 1942 that the first successful flight was made with the preferred Junkers Jumo 003 turbojets installed – the BMW 003 had initially been trialled, but persistent failures had seen it discarded in early 1942. With the engine/airframe combination at last sorted out, political interference from no less a figure than the *Führer* himself saw the programme side-tracked for a number of months as he insisted that the aircraft be developed as a bomber. Sense finally prevailed in early 1944, and the first aircraft to reach the frontline saw combat in June of that year. Despite Germany being bombed virtually 24 hours a day during the final 12 months of the war, 1400+ Me 262s were completed by Messerschmitt, and a further 500 were lost in air raids. Engine reliability, fuel shortages and unrealistic operational taskings restricted the frontline force to around 200 jets at any one time, but these nevertheless accounted for over 200 Allied aircraft (*Jagdwaffe* claims exceeded 745 victories for the Me 262!) during day and night interceptions. A total of 28 pilots 'made ace' flying the jet with the seven units that saw combat.

Me 262A-1a Wk-Nr 110559/'Red 13' of Oberstleutnant Heinz Bär, *Kommandeur* III./EJG 2, Lager-Lechfeld, March 1945

One of the last of a long line of 'lucky 13s' flown by Heinz Bär during a distinguished and incident-packed career, this aircraft wears an upper surface camouflage combination of dark brown and bright medium green over pale blue undersides. Beginning with a French Hawk H-75A downed on 25 September 1939, Bär had amassed 204 piston-engined aerial victories before transitioning to the

Me 262, on which he scored a further 16 to become the leading daylight jet ace, and second only to the nightfighting Kurt Welter in the overall rankings.

HERO OF THE SOVIET UNION

'Faced with a real opponent in the heat of the battle, a fighter pilot had to have willpower, stamina and an unshakeable determination to destroy his target.'

Kapitan Sergei Dolgushin (left), squadron leader with 32.Gu.IAP, poses with his regiment commander, Col Vasili Stalin, during the winter of 1943 (*via Nigel Eastaway*)

Whilst supporting the final push towards Berlin in 1945, Lt Col Sergei Dolgushin of the 156th Fighter Regiment (IAP), 215th Fighter Aviation Division (IAD), 8th Aviation Army Corps (IAK) claims yet another kill in his Lavochkin La-7 'White 93'.

Despite attaining high rank and scoring at least 28 personal kills, Dolgushin enjoyed a somewhat chequered career. During the mid-war years, whilst serving as a senior member of the La-5/La-5FN-equipped 32nd Guards Fighter Regiment (Gu.IAP), Dolgushin (and fellow ace Valentin Bobkov) was transferred to another unit as a disciplinary measure following a fishing expedition in which the regiment's engineering officer was blown up by an 82 mm rocket! Two pilots were also injured, including the CO of 32.Gu.IAP, Vasili Stalin (son of Joseph Stalin no less), who was removed from his post as a result of this incident.

Although the secrets to Dolgushin's combat success have so far failed to make it into print, fellow ace Aleksandr Pokryshkin gave the following pointers on how fighter pilots of the Red Air Force went about defeating their highly skilled Luftwaffe opponents on the Eastern Front;

'The main thing was to have a creative approach to any air combat. Without speed you could not make that tricky turn, gain height, make the surprise attack or get in the decisive burst of fire. What did we achieve if we built up a good turn of speed? First of all suddenness of attack. In warfare, seconds could be priceless, and a split-second could decide an outcome. Speed enabled all the attention to be concentrated on looking for the enemy ahead, speed resulting not only from engine power but from altitude.

'After analysing dozens of air combats, and having studied the outcome and interrelationships between the elements of fighting in the dive and climb, I came to the conclusion that height gave you the opportunity to take up a more favourable position for your attack, improved your field of vision and enabled you to build up a high speed in a dive, which in turn assisted you to carry out your "vertical" manoeuvre. All this created favourable conditions for a decisive surprise attack, and made it easier to break away afterwards.

'As for firepower, the essence of this component of the formula was its efficacy. You had to hit the enemy from close in, thus ensuring a good chance of hitting without wasting ammunition. The dispersal of bullets and shells at a range of 300 metres was at that time so great that only a few got home – and then without any penetrating power. You had to get in close and open fire from around 100 metres, or often closer. Faced with a real opponent in the heat of the battle, a fighter pilot had to have willpower, stamina and an unshakeable determination to destroy his target. Only then could you hit the target.'

From the German perspective, Soviet success in combat in the final two years of the war often stemmed from the sheer number of aircraft they could put into the air in support of troops and tanks pushing westward. The *Experten* took a heavy toll of these red-starred fighters and bombers, and none more so than the world's most successful ace with 352 kills, Erich Hartmann;

'Often there were ten of us against 300 Russians. Those are long odds. A mid-air collision was almost as likely as being shot down, too. We had to plan our attacks against these hordes with great care or we never would have survived.'

LEFT S F Dolgushin, S V Makarov and N N Borovoi all flew MiG-3s with 180.IAP during late 1941, this shot being taken at the unit's Borky airfield, on the West Front, in November of that year. Sergei Makarov was a prewar pilot who scored heavily until he was lost in action in an I-16 with 728.IAP on the Kalinin Front on 10 February 1942. He claimed 23 kills (13 shared) and was awarded the HSU prior to his death (*via Nigel Eastaway*)

BOTTOM Dolgushin was commanding 156.IAP when the regiment converted from the thoroughly obsolete LaGG-3 to the La-5 in the autumn of 1943. After conversion, the unit was assigned to 215.IAD of 8.IAK, and was held in reserve for over six months. Indeed, it was not until June 1944 that 156.IAP relocated to Belorussia to take part in the Bobruisk operation (*via Nigel Eastaway*)

BELOW By late 1944, 156.IAP had been reassigned to the 4th Air Army along with the rest of 8.IAK, re-equipped with La-7s, and participated in the liberation of Belorussia and Poland. Dolgushin's most famous La-7 was 'White 93', which was lost in February 1945 when its engine was hit by flak over Danzig. Fortunately, the ace was able to reach his own lines before making a forced landing. Issued with 'White 14' in its place, Dolgushin continued flying combat missions through to the very end of the war in Europe – his final wartime sortie took place on 6 May 1945 (*via Phil Jarrett*)

PILOT BIOGRAPHY – SERGEI DOLGUSHIN

Born on 25 September 1920 in Novopokrovskoe, in the Tula Region of Russia, to a peasant family, Sergei Dolgushin worked in a factory while studying at an aeroclub in the late 1930s. Joining the army in 1939, he graduated from the Kacha Flight School the following year. Small of stature, blond, blue-eyed and of a cheerful disposition, Dolgushin was recognised as a natural pilot from the earliest days of the war.

He had a long and varied operational career, serving initially with the I-16-equipped 122.IAP at the time of the German invasion of the Soviet Union on 22 June 1941. Seeing action right from the start of Operation *Barbarossa*, Dolgushin transferred to 180.IAP on the West Front in August, having already scored a handful of kills. By February of 1942 he had flown 185 sorties and claimed 11 kills, and was made a Hero of the Soviet Union (HSU) three months later. In June of that year his regiment re-equipped with Hurricanes, and he claimed at least four kills with the British fighter prior to moving to the Yak-7B-equipped 434.IAP in August 1942. Soon renamed 32.Gu.IAP, this regiment saw extensive action on the Kalinin Front. Dolgushin, who had been promoted to *kapitan* and given command of an *eskadrilya*, scored a further six victories with 32.Gu.IAP.

Transferred to 30.Gu.IAP following the infamous fishing expedition of June 1943, he had flown P-39s with this regiment for just four months when he was given command of 156.IAP. Now flying the La-5N, and then the La-7, Dolgushin remained in charge of the regiment right through to VE-Day. During his time in command, 156.IAP supported the liberation of Belorussia and Poland, before seeing action over northern Germany in the last months of the war. Dolgushin's final official victory tally stood at 17 individual and 11 shared kills, but to this should be added four individual claims denied him by his first regimental commissar (due to a clash of personalities!) in 1941.

After the war, he commanded a number of fighter and bomber regiments, prior to attending the General Staff academy. Dolgushin eventually became the deputy commander of an air army, being promoted to lieutenant-general in 1967. He finally retired from the air force in 1976.

La-7 'White 93' of Lt Col Sergei Dolgushin, Commander of 156.IAP, 215.IAD, 8.IAK, Germany, early 1945

Sergei Dolgushin's distinctively marked La-7 had its upper surfaces painted in medium grey overall and the undersurfaces standard light blue. The nose was red as far as the second aluminium cowling band, and the gold star and red ribbon of the HSU were painted on the left side of the cowling. The red nose was adopted as a Corps air marking in September 1944 in response to an order issued by the commander of 8.IAK. Beneath the cockpit on the port side were four rows of victory stars, with the 17 in red denoting individual kills and the 11 in white shared victories. At the top of the fin was a small yellow Cyrillic letter in the shape of a reversed capital E, which signified 156.IAP's honorific designation 'Elbinskii', or Elbe, whilst to the right of it was the La-7's white factory marking.

SPECIFICATION

Lavochkin La-5/7
(all dimensions and performance data for La-7)

TYPE:	single-engined monoplane fighter
ACCOMMODATION:	pilot
DIMENSIONS:	length 29 ft 2.5 in (8.90 m)
	wingspan 32 ft 1.75 in (9.80 m)
	height 0 ft 6.25 in (2.60 m)
WEIGHTS:	empty 5842 lb (2620 kg)
	maximum take-off 7496 lb (3400 kg)
PERFORMANCE:	maximum speed 423 mph (680 kmh)
	range 615 miles (990 km)
	powerplant Shvetsov M-82FN
	output 1850 hp (1380 kW)
ARMAMENT:	two or three 20 mm cannon in upper cowling;
	provision for bombs or rockets under wings
FIRST FLIGHT DATE:	March 1942 (La-5)
OPERATORS:	Czechoslovakia, USSR
PRODUCTION:	9920 La-5s and 5753 La-7s

The first Lavochkin-designed fighter to see series production was the LaGG-3, which despite being one of the most modern fighters in the Soviet arsenal in June 1941, was not a match for the Luftwaffe fighters of the day. Underpowered and less manoeuvrable than the Bf 109F/G or Fw 190A, hundreds of LaGG-3s fell to the *Jagdwaffe*. Stunned by reports of the fighter's combat inadequacies, Lavochkin swiftly replaced the aircraft's inline M-105PF engine with the far more powerful Shvetsov M-82 radial in early 1942. The resulting fighter proved to be not only faster than its predecessor, but also more capable at medium to high altitudes. Designated the La-5, the first examples to reach the frontline (during the battle for Stalingrad in late 1942) were actually re-engined LaGG-3s. By late March 1943 production of the definitive La-5N had commenced, this variant featuring a fuel-injected M-82FN for better performance at altitude and cut down rear fuselage decking and a new canopy for better all round vision. The La-5FN was more than a match for the Bf 109G, and could hold its own with the Fw 190. In November 1943 the further improved La-7 started flight trials, this model boasting even greater performance thanks to the lightening of its overall structure and adoption of the metal wing spars featured in late-build La-5FNs. Attention was also paid to reducing the fighter's drag coefficient, which resulted in the adoption of a revised cowling and inboard wing leading edge surfaces. The La-7 entered service in the spring of 1944, and went on to become the favoured mount of many Soviet aces.

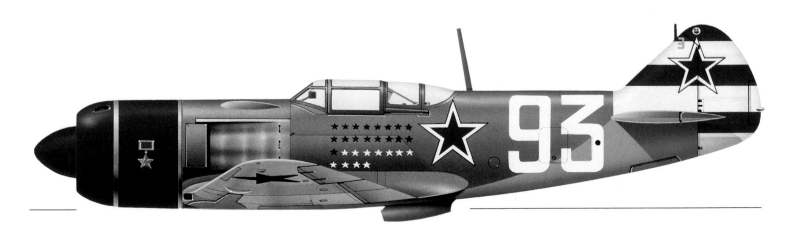

'MASTER FALCON'

'It was easy for us to shoot these P-51s down, for their sole defensive manoeuvre was to perform a circular turn.'

'At around 1000 hrs on 16 July 1945, we received information about enemy movement – there was a group of small aircraft flying towards Ise Bay, near Nagoya. My group had 12 aircraft, consisting of Sugiyama flight (four aircraft), Mihara flight (four aircraft) and my flight (four aircraft). Eto group also had 12 aircraft, and we took off together that morning to fight the approaching P-51s.

'Flying high, I kept my aircraft above and to the right of the Eto group. We flew over Shinmiya and then turned left, flying along the coastline heading for Shimahanto. At an altitude of about 7000 metres, just above Ise shrine, Sugiyama flight turned to the right toward the ocean, and the distance between our flights and Eto's group grew. Then we sighted the P-51 group flying well below us just above the ocean. They looked so small, just like floating strings.

'All of a sudden, Sugiyama flight headed downward straight into the P-51s. I sped up in order to stay with them, and to provide cover for their attack. I saw the P-51 group make a sudden turn. There were eleven aircraft in three flights. I approached the last plane with the thought of revenge for my leg, which I had lost in Burma. I noticed that my aircraft was sliding around a lot because of a propeller problem that arose when I opened the throttle.

'Despite pressing my artificial leg hard down against the rudder pedal, I still felt frustration at not having any real control over this limb. I dived down on the enemy plane, and at a distance of no

Lt Hinoki prepares to board his extremely weathered 64th Sentai Ki-43-Ic in Malaya in 1942. Like many Japanese Army Air Force (JAAF) officer pilots, he would often carry his sword in his aircraft for good luck. Hinoki's flight helmet was a gift from his instructor, Nomonhan ace Maj Iwori Sakai (*via Yohei Hinoki*)

Iain Wyllie

This Ki-100-Ib *Goshikisen* of the Akeno Fighter School was flown by 1Lt Mamoru Tatsuda on the famous 16 July 1945 dogfight over Nagoya Bay, when the instructor's flight (1st Daitai) was led into combat against P-51Ds of the 457th and 458th FSs by Maj Yohei Hinoki. This photograph was taken at Komaki airfield on 13 August 1945. The Ki-100 was considered by many to have been the best JAAF fighter of the war (*via Yohei Hinoki*)

Having only been with the 64th Sentai a matter of weeks, a young Lt Hinoki poses with his Ki-43-I at Ipoh airfield, in Malaya. He had already claimed two Hurricanes and a Blenheim destroyed by the time this photo was taken in early 1942 (*via Yohei Hinoki*)

more than 20 metres, I opened fire. I fired several times and the aircraft soon dived away out of control. It was easy for us to shoot these P-51s down, for their sole defensive manoeuvre was to perform a circular turn. The Ki-100 had a superior turning circle in comparison with the P-51, and we simply cut inside their defensive turns.

'The enemy planes had come to attack the Kyuko area, but they were forced to alter their mission due to our interception. Our 24 aircraft had intercepted around 250 American planes, and we would have easily won this fight if we had had more experienced pilots within our group. In order to prevail, we had to fight as a group, but instead we fought individually and lost three great pilots.

'I soon found myself alone surrounded by 15 aircraft, all of which were shooting at me. I made a series of sharp circular turns in an effort to avoid being hit. When I decided to withdraw, the leader of the enemy aircraft that surrounded me commenced a series of aggressive manoeuvres in an effort to finish me off. I responded with a sequence of tight circular turns, but soon realised that I couldn't escape. In desperation, I pushed my plane over into a vertical dive and opened the throttles. Despite my body being subjected to an incredible build up of air pressure, the aircraft remained fully controllable, and when I pulled out of the dive I was totally alone. The fight had lasted a full 50 minutes.

'We destroyed 11 enemy aircraft, but lost three pilots in return. Considering that our small team was only newly-assembled, and fighting against such a large group of enemy aircraft, the loss of three pilots was not so bad. We owed this result principally to our aircraft, which we called the *Goshikisen*.'

These Ki-100-I-Ko *Goshikisen* of the 1st Chutai of the 59th Sentai sit in readiness for a rapid scramble from Ashiya Airfield in Fukuoka Prefecture, Japan, in June 1945. Known as the 'Tony II', the Ki-100 was basically a Ki-61 airframe mated to a Mitsubishi Ha-112-II 14-cylinder air-cooled radial engine. The Ki-100-I-Ko was the most common *Goshikisen* of them all, with some 272 airframes having been built by war's end (*via Henry Sakaida*)

SPECIFICATION

Kawasaki Ki-100 *Goshikisen*
(all dimensions and performance data for Ki-100-I)

TYPE:	single-engined monoplane fighter
ACCOMMODATION:	pilot
DIMENSIONS:	length 28 ft 11.25 in (8.82 m)
	wingspan 39 ft 4.5 in (12.00 m)
	height 12 ft 3.5 in (3.75 m)
WEIGHTS:	empty 5567 lb (2525 kg)
	maximum take-off 7705 lb (3495 kg)
PERFORMANCE:	maximum speed 360 mph (579 kmh)
	range 1367 miles (2200 km) with external tanks
	powerplant Mitsubishi Ha-112-II
	output 1500 hp (1118 kW)
ARMAMENT:	two 20 mm cannon in nose and two 12.7 mm machine guns in wings; provision for two 551-lb (250-kg) bombs under wings
FIRST FLIGHT DATE:	1 February 1945
OPERATORS:	Japan
PRODUCTION:	396

PILOT BIOGRAPHY – YOHEI HINOKI

Yohei Hinoki was born in Tokushima Prefecture in 1919. He received his flight commission in June 1941 and was posted to the 64th Sentai, where he served in the Malayan campaign flying the Ki-43 Hayabusa.

On the opening day of the war Hinoki fought against No 34 Sqn Blenheim IVs, claiming a half-share in the destruction of one of the bombers. Assigned as wingman to Sentai commander Maj Tateo Kato, his job was to protect his commander at all costs. Opportunities to engage in free-for-all combat were therefore rather rare, but Hinoki did, nevertheless, manage to claim two No 238 Sqn Hurricane IIs shot down over Singapore on 31 January 1942.

On 10 April 1942 AVG P-40Cs clashed with the 64th Sentai over Loiwing, China, in a low altitude dogfight in the clouds. Hinoki became embroiled in a fierce tussle with 3rd AVG Sqn ace Flt Ldr Robert T Smith. The Hayabusa pilot was seriously wounded in the left arm and buttocks during the clash, his parachute harness stopping a 0.50 in round from lodging in his back.

On 25 November 1943 Hinoki may have become the first Japanese pilot to shoot down a P-51 (probably an A-36A) in the CBI. Two days later he was struck by a 0.50 in bullet when engaging more Mustangs, and had to have his leg amputated soon after he landed. He subsequently spent many months in the base hospital gaining sufficient strength in order to survive being shipped back to Japan.

Because of his invaluable combat experience, Hinoki became an instructor at the Akeno Fighter School, and fitted with an artificial leg, he later went on to flying combat missions in the Ki-100 against B-29s and their escorts.

It is estimated that Maj Yohei Hinoki downed more than 12 aircraft, and his varied combat experiences demonstrated that a skilled pilot in a lightly-armed fighter like the Hayabusa could destroy Hurricanes, Lightnings, Mustangs and even Liberators. The 'Master Falcon' passed away in January 1991.

Considered by many to be Japan's best fighter of the war, the Ki-100 was born out of an urgent need for an aircraft that could intercept AAF B-29s raiding the home islands at altitudes of around 30,000 ft. The Ki-61-II-KAI had originally been designed to fill this requirement, but chronic problems with its inline Ha-140 powerplant resulted in over 200 airframes being left idle on the ground devoid of engines. In November 1944 Kawasaki was ordered by the Japanese Ministry of Munitions to install a replacement engine, and after some searching, the Mitsubishi Ha-112 radial was chosen. Engineers studied the engine mountings of an imported Fw 190A to see how their German counterparts had mated a 'fat' radial to a slim fuselage. Armed with this knowledge, work proceeded swiftly on the Ki-100-I, and 271 airframes were fitted with the Mitsubishi engine between March and June 1945. The new fighter came as an unpleasant surprise to the Americans, with Japanese pilots immediately enjoying success not only against the feared B-29s, but also Hellcats, Mustangs and Corsairs. Aside from being a joy to fly, the Ki-100 also proved immensely popular with long-suffering groundcrews, many of whom had been struggling with the Ki-61's Ha-40/140 for longer than they cared to remember. Finally, an all-new version of the Ki-100 entered production in May 1945, the -Ib featuring cut-down rear fuselage decking and an all-round vision canopy.

Ki-100-Ib of Maj Yohei Hinoki, leader of the 1st Daitai, Akeno Fighter School, Komaki, July 1945

Maj Hinoki was flying this aircraft (one of only 106 production-standard Ki-100-Ibs ever built) when he downed the P-51D flown by Capt John W Benbow of the 457th

FS/506th FG on 16 July 1945. The AAF pilot was leading the second element of Capt William B Lawrence's flight when Hinoki closed to within 20 metres of his target and delivered the fatal blow – the latter was forced to attack from such close range due to severe propeller vibration ruling out the accurate use of his gunsight. On this day, the AAF's Seventh Fighter Command sortied the 21st and 506th FGs from Iwo Jima on a long-range mission to Japan to attack airfields in the Nagoya area.

APPENDICES

AIRCRAFT OF THE ACES

Titles published to date

AIRCRAFT OF THE ACES 1
• MUSTANG ACES OF THE EIGHTH
AIR FORCE • ISBN 1 85532 447 4

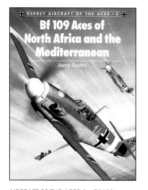

AIRCRAFT OF THE ACES 2 • Bf 109
ACES OF NORTH AFRICA AND THE
MEDITERRANEAN • ISBN 1 85532 448 2

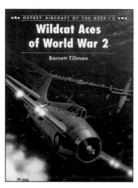

AIRCRAFT OF THE ACES 3
• WILDCAT ACES OF WORLD WAR 2
• ISBN 1 85532 486 5

AIRCRAFT OF THE ACES 4
• KOREAN WAR ACES
• ISBN 1 85532 501 2

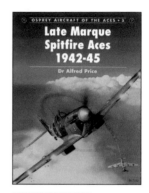

AIRCRAFT OF THE ACES 5
• LATE MARQUE SPITFIRE ACES 1942-45
• ISBN 1 85532 575 6

AIRCRAFT OF THE ACES 6
• FOCKE-WULF Fw 190 ACES OF THE
RUSSIAN FRONT • ISBN 1 85532 518 7

AIRCRAFT OF THE ACES 7
• MUSTANG ACES OF THE 9th & 15th AIR
FORCES & THE RAF • ISBN 1 85532 583 7

AIRCRAFT OF THE ACES 8
• CORSAIR ACES OF WORLD WAR 2
• ISBN 1 85532 530 6

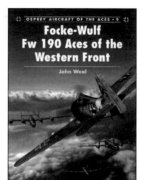

AIRCRAFT OF THE ACES 9
• FOCKE-WULF Fw 190 ACES OF THE
WESTERN FRONT • ISBN 1 85532 595 0

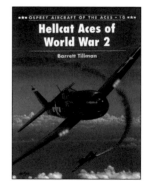

AIRCRAFT OF THE ACES 10
• HELLCAT ACES OF WORLD WAR 2
• ISBN 1 85532 596 9

AIRCRAFT OF THE ACES 11
• Bf 109D/E ACES 1939-41
• ISBN 1 85532 487 3

AIRCRAFT OF THE ACES 12
• SPITFIRE MARK I/II ACES 1939-41
• ISBN 1 85532 627 2

AIRCRAFT OF THE ACES 13
• JAPANESE ARMY AIR FORCE ACES
1937-45 • ISBN 1 85532 529 2

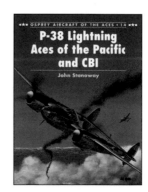

AIRCRAFT OF THE ACES 14
• P-38 LIGHTNING ACES OF THE PACIFIC
AND CBI • ISBN 1 85532 633 7

AIRCRAFT OF THE ACES 15
• SOVIET ACES OF WORLD WAR 2
• ISBN 1 85532 632 9

AIRCRAFT OF THE ACES 16
• SPITFIRE MARK V ACES 1941-45
• ISBN 1 85532 635 3

AIRCRAFT OF THE ACES 17
• GERMAN JET ACES OF WORLD WAR 2
• ISBN 1 85532 634 5

AIRCRAFT OF THE ACES 18
• HURRICANE ACES 1939-40
• ISBN 1 85532 597 7

AIRCRAFT OF THE ACES 19
• P-38 LIGHTNING ACES OF THE
ETO/MTO • ISBN 1 85532 698 1

AIRCRAFT OF THE ACES 20
• GERMAN NIGHT FIGHTER ACES OF
WORLD WAR 2 • ISBN 1 85532 696 5

AIRCRAFT OF THE ACES 21
• POLISH ACES OF WORLD WAR 2
• ISBN 1 85532 726 0

AIRCRAFT OF THE ACES 22
• IMPERIAL JAPANESE NAVY ACES
1937-45 • ISBN 1 85532 727 9

AIRCRAFT OF THE ACES 23
• FINNISH ACES OF WORLD WAR 2
• ISBN 1 85532 783 X

AIRCRAFT OF THE ACES 24
• P-47 THUNDERBOLT ACES OF THE
EIGHTH AIR FORCE • ISBN 1 85532 729 5

AIRCRAFT OF THE ACES 25 • MESSER-
SCHMITT Bf 110 ZERSTÖRER ACES OF
WORLD WAR 2 • ISBN 1 85532 753 8

AIRCRAFT OF THE ACES 26 • MUSTANG
AND THUNDERBOLT ACES OF THE
PACIFIC AND CBI • ISBN 1 85532 780 5

AIRCRAFT OF THE ACES 27
• TYPHOON/TEMPEST ACES OF
WORLD WAR 2 • ISBN 1 85532 779 1

AIRCRAFT OF THE ACES 28
• FRENCH ACES OF WORLD WAR 2
• ISBN 1 85532 898 4

AIRCRAFT OF THE ACES 29
• Bf 109F/G/K ACES OF THE WESTERN
FRONT • ISBN 1 85532 905 0

AIRCRAFT OF THE ACES 30 • P-47
THUNDERBOLT ACES OF THE NINTH AND
FIFTEENTH AIR FORCES • ISBN 1 85532 906 9

AIRCRAFT OF THE ACES 31 (SPECIAL)
• VIII FIGHTER COMMAND AT WAR
• ISBN 1 85532 907 7
(NOT AVAILABLE UNTIL 9/2000)

AIRCRAFT OF THE ACES 32
• ALBATROS ACES OF WORLD WAR 1
• ISBN 1 85532 960 3

AIRCRAFT OF THE ACES 33
• NIEUPORT ACES OF WORLD WAR 1
• ISBN 1 85532 961 1

THE AIRCRAFT OF THE ACES

All of the drawings featured over the next four pages are reproduced to 1/72nd scale

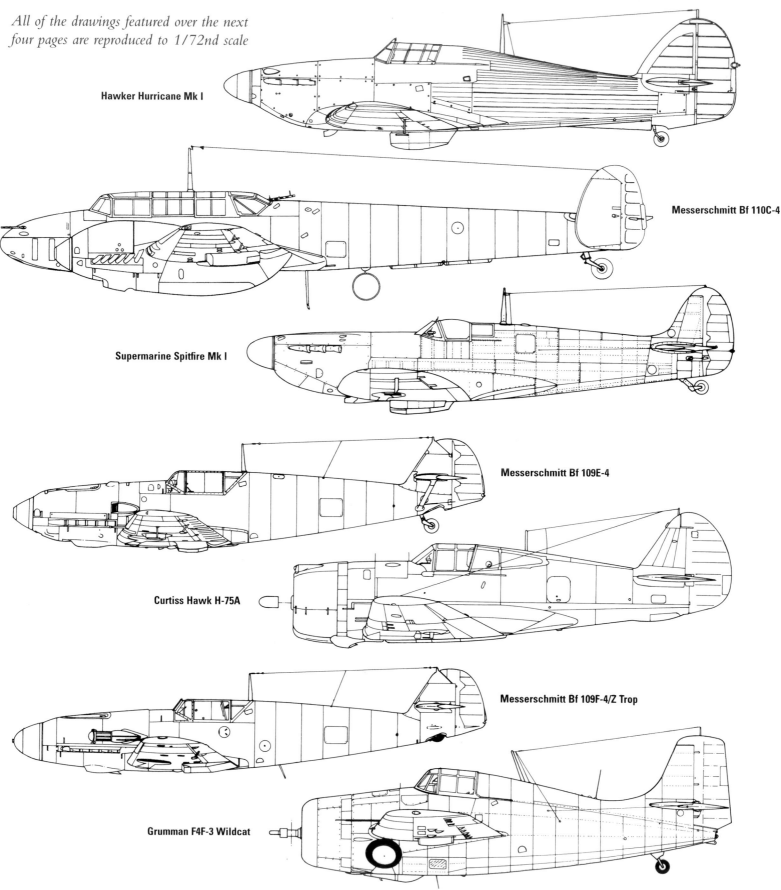

Hawker Hurricane Mk I

Messerschmitt Bf 110C-4

Supermarine Spitfire Mk I

Messerschmitt Bf 109E-4

Curtiss Hawk H-75A

Messerschmitt Bf 109F-4/Z Trop

Grumman F4F-3 Wildcat

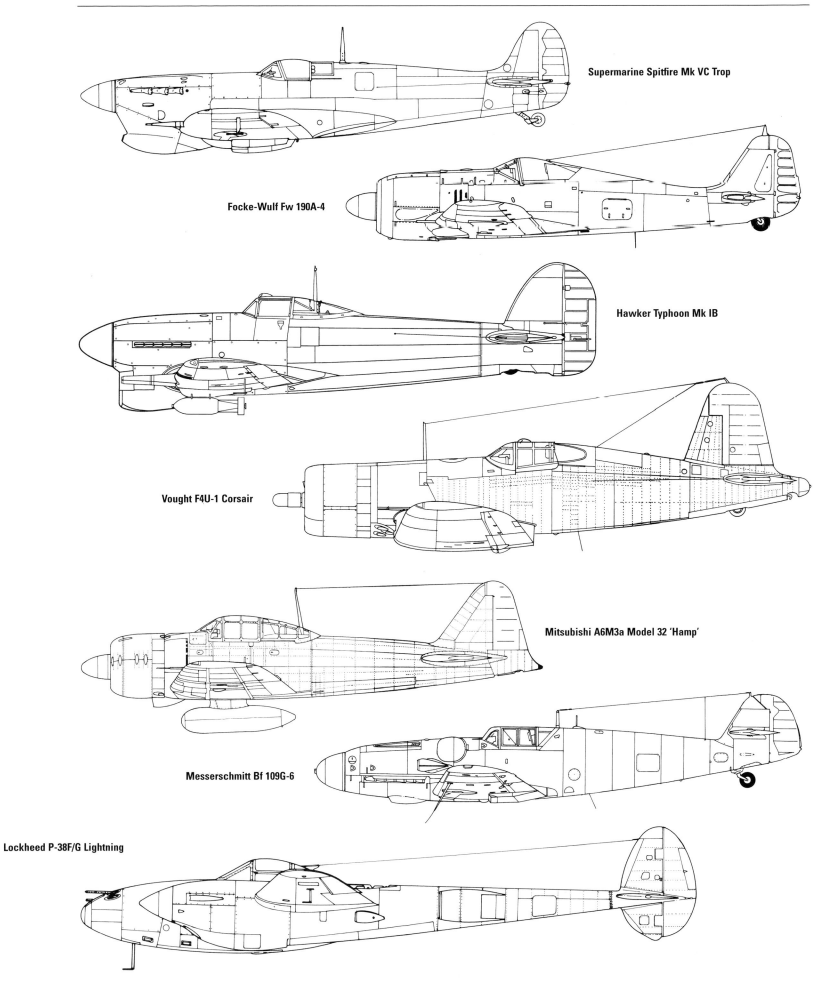

Supermarine Spitfire Mk VC Trop

Focke-Wulf Fw 190A-4

Hawker Typhoon Mk IB

Vought F4U-1 Corsair

Mitsubishi A6M3a Model 32 'Hamp'

Messerschmitt Bf 109G-6

Lockheed P-38F/G Lightning

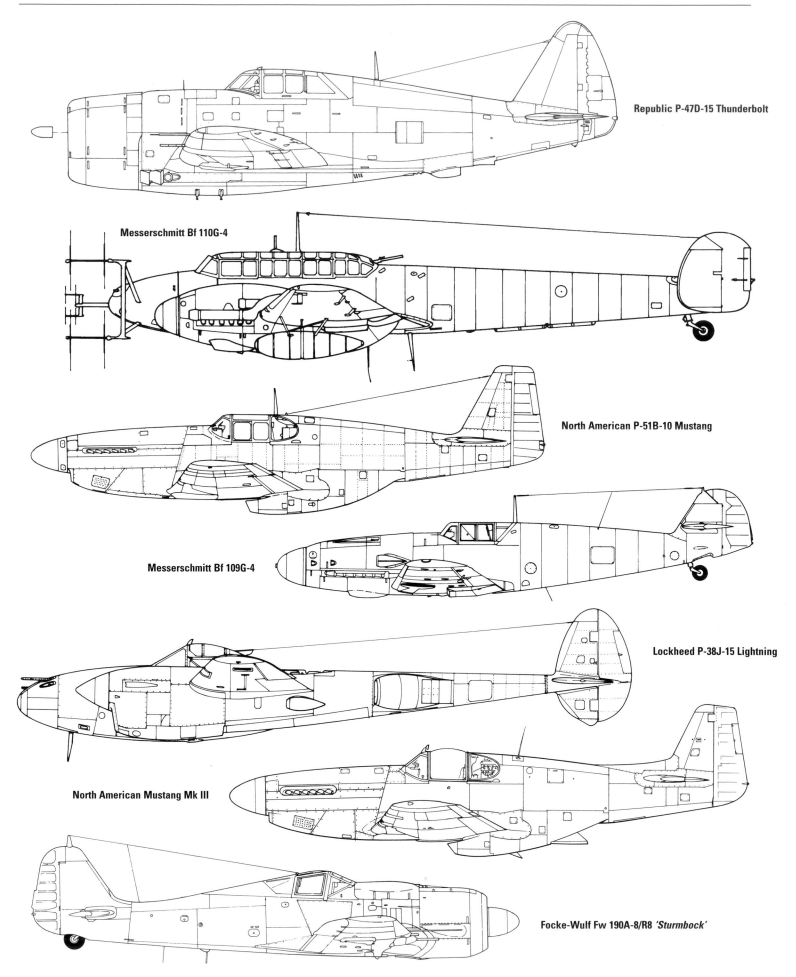

Republic P-47D-15 Thunderbolt

Messerschmitt Bf 110G-4

North American P-51B-10 Mustang

Messerschmitt Bf 109G-4

Lockheed P-38J-15 Lightning

North American Mustang Mk III

Focke-Wulf Fw 190A-8/R8 *'Sturmbock'*

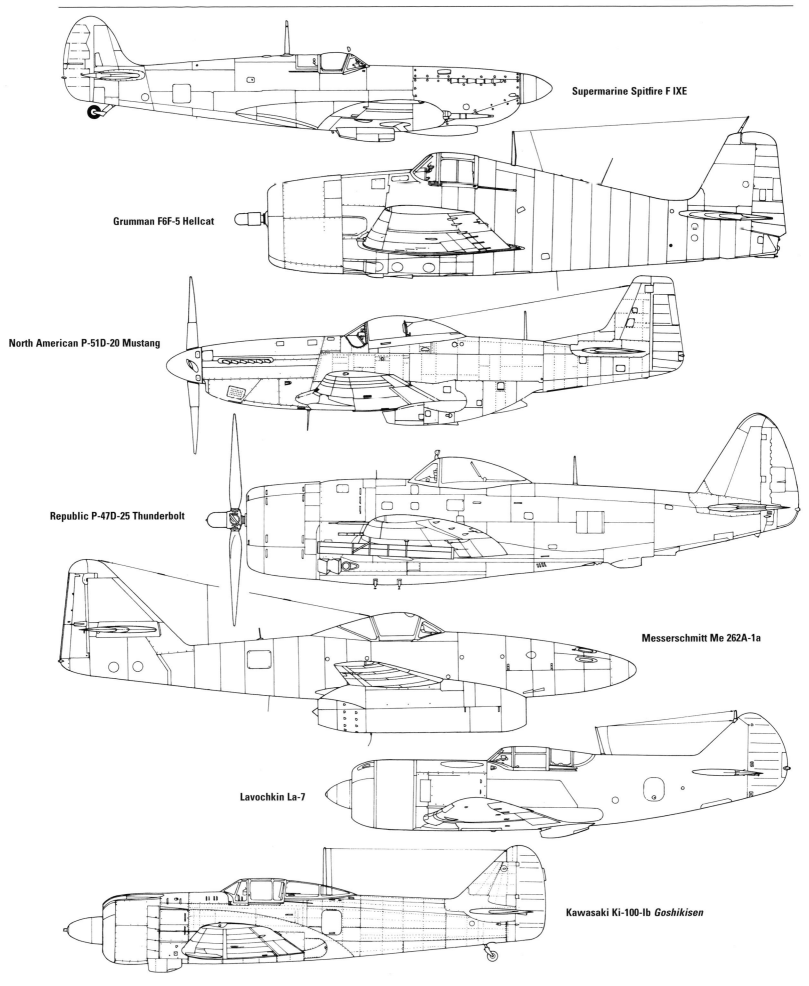

Supermarine Spitfire F IXE

Grumman F6F-5 Hellcat

North American P-51D-20 Mustang

Republic P-47D-25 Thunderbolt

Messerschmitt Me 262A-1a

Lavochkin La-7

Kawasaki Ki-100-Ib *Goshikisen*

TOP FIGHTER ACES OF WORLD WAR 2

AXIS

GERMANY

Erich Hartmann 352
Gerhard Barkhorn 301
Gunther Rall 275
Otto Kittel 267
Walter Nowotny 258
Wilhelm Batz 237

FINLAND

Ilmari Juutilainen 94
Hans Wind 75
Eino Luukkanen 56
Urho Lehtovaara 44.5
Oiva Tuominen 44
Olli Puhakka 42

HUNGARY

Dezsö Szentgyörgyi 34
György Debrödy 26
Laszlo Molnar 25
Lajos Toth 24
Mikos Kenyeres 19
Istvan Fabian 13

RUMANIA

Prince Constantine
   Cantacuzene 60
Alexandre Serbanescu 50
Florian Budu 40
Jon Milu 18

CROATIA

Vitan Galic 36
Mato Dubovak 34
Jan Gerthofer 33
Isidor Kovaric 28
Jan Reznak 26
Mato Culinovic 18

ITALY

Franco Lucchini 26
   (including 5 in Spanish
   Civil War)
Adriano Visconti 26
   (including 5 with RSI)

Leonardo Ferrulli 22
   (including 1 in Spanish
   Civil War)
Teresio Martinoli 22
Franco Bordoni-Bisleri 19
Luigi Gorrini 19
   (including 4 with RSI)

JAPAN

NAVAL AIR FORCE
   (ALL TALLIES UNVERIFIED)

Tetsuzo Iwamoto 202
   (14 in China in 1938)
Shoichi Sugita 120+
Hiroyoshi Nishizawa 86
Shigeo Fukumoto 72
Saburo Sakai 60+
   (2 in China in 1938-39)
Takeo Okumura 54
   (4 in China in 1940)

ARMY AIR FORCE
   (ALL TALLIES UNVERIFIED)

Hiromichi Shinohara 58
   (all in China in 1939)
Yashiko Kuroe 51
   (2 in China in 1939)
Satoshi Anabuki 51
Toshio Sakagawa 49+
Yoshihiko Nakada 45
Kenji Shimada 40
   (all in China in 1939)

ALLIED

USA

ARMY AIR FORCE

Richard Bong 40
Thomas McGuire 38
Francis Gabreski 28
   (plus 6.50 in Korea)
Robert Johnson 27
Charles MacDonald 27
George Preddy 26.83

US NAVY

David McCampbell 34
Cecil Harris 24
Eugene Valencia 23
Patrick Fleming 19
Alexander Vraciu 19
Cornelius Nooy 18

US MARINE CORPS

Joseph Foss 26
Robert Hanson 25
Gregory Boyington 22
   (plus 2 with AVG)
Kenneth Walsh 21
Donald Aldrich 20
John Smith 19

BELGIUM

Count Rodolphe de Hemricourt
   de Grunne 13
   (including 5 in Spanish
   Civil War)
Count Ivan Du Monceau
   de Bergendael 8
Jean Offenberg 7
Charles Detal 6.50
Remi van Lierde 6 (and 40 V1s)
Victor Ortmans 6

CZECHOSLOVAKIA

Karel Kuttelwascher 20
Josef Frantisek 18
Alois Vasatko 12.333
Frantisek Perina 11
Morislav Mansfeld 8.75
   (and 2 V1s)
Otto Smik 8 (and 3 V1s)

FRANCE
(OFFICIAL *ARMÉE DEL l'AIR* LIST)

Pierre Clostermann 33
Marcel Albert 23
Jean Demozay (Morlaix) 21
Pierre Le Gloan 18
Jacques André 16
Louis Delfino 16

GREAT BRITAIN

Marmaduke St John Pattle
   (South African) 52
James Johnson (English) 41
Adolf Malan (South African) 34
William Vale (English) 33
George Beurling (Canadian) 32
Brendan Finucane (Irish) 32

POLAND

Stanislaw Skalski 21
Witold Urbanowicz 18
   (plus 1 in 1936)
Boleslaw Gladych 17
Eugeniusz Horbaczewski 17
Marian Pisarek 13
Jan Zumbach 13

NORWAY

Sven Heglund 14.50
Werner Christie 11
Helmer Grundt-Spang 10.33
Martin Gran 9.50
Marius Eriksen 9

SOVIET UNION

Lev Shestako 65
   (including 39 victories in
   Spain and 42 shared victories
   in total)
Ivan Kozhedub 62
Grigorii Rechkalov 61
   (including 5 group victories)
Nikolai Gulayev 60
   (including 3 group victories)
Aleksandr Pokryshkin 59
   (including 6 group victories)
Aleksei Alelyukhin 57
   (including 17 group victories)

CHINA

Liu Chi-Sun 11.333 (1937-41)
Wang Kuang-Fu 8.50 (1944-45)
Kao Yu-hsin 8
Kuan Tan 8 (1944-45)
Yuan Pao-Kang 8 (1937-38)
Chow Che-Kei 6 (1944)